# No One's Child

*Thank you for reading*

## Esther Asher

Sarah Grace
Publishing
Dyslexic Friendly

# Endorsements

"This is one of the most profound, raw pieces of writing about human trafficking I have ever read. Esther describes her heart-breaking experience of being stripped of all humanity, dignity and empathy as her childhood and innocence were brutally stolen from her. Hers is a difficult but essential story for us to hear and by which to have our hearts changed so that we may join in the fight to end this horrific crime of sex trafficking, which victimises two million children a year, and twenty million adults. Each one of those lives is worth our attention, each worth our efforts to pull them out of this literal hell or prevent them from being dragged there in the first place. Esther's rise from the trauma and pain of her past is a testament to the human spirit and the very real potential for all survivors of human trafficking to regain the lives they were born for. She is a phoenix and inspires us all to help everyone still in bondage to rise with her."

Mira Sorvino
*UNODC Goodwill Ambassador in the worldwide fight against trafficking in persons*

"A true tale of perseverance in its highest form, Esther's story is one of overcoming and freedom that you'll never forget!"

Rebecca Bender
*CEO and Founder, Elevate Academy, author and speaker*

# Disclaimer

This book contains personal accounts of sex trafficking, abuse, trauma and recovery. The experiences shared within are deeply personal and may be distressing to some readers. While these events have been recounted with honesty and integrity, readers are advised that certain names, locations and identifying details have been changed to protect the privacy and safety of those involved.

This autobiography is intended to shed light on the realities of trafficking, raise awareness, and offer hope and strength to those who may be facing similar circumstances. It is not meant to sensationalise trauma, but to honour survival, resilience and the journey towards healing.

Reader discretion is strongly advised.

# Acknowledgements

I would like to thank everyone for supporting and loving me throughout the years of recovery and the journey of writing this book.

First published 2025 by Sarah Grace Publishing,
an imprint of
Malcolm Down Publishing Ltd.
www.sarahgracepublishing.co.uk
www.malcolmdown.co.uk

29 28 27 26 25  7 6 5 4 3 2 1

British Library Cataloguing in Publication Data
A catalogue record for this book is available
from the British Library.

ISBN 978-1-917455-18-3

Cover design by Esther Kotecha
Art direction by Sarah Grace

Printed in the UK

# No One's Child

When I took my first breath,
There was no air.
When I took my first steps,
There was no one to cheer.
When I said my first word,
No one heard it.
When I had my first bad dream,
No one soothed me.
When I bruised my knees on the playground,
There was no one to wipe my tears.
On my first day of school,
No one was proud.
The first time I was picked on,
No one stood up for me.
First time I was pushed,
No one cared.
First time my heart broke,
I held the pieces.
When I got my first job,
No one felt joy.
With my first suicide attempt,
The bedside was empty.
At the first sign of trouble,
No one wanted to know me.
The first time I cried for help,
No one cared enough to listen.
Why?
Am I no one's child?

# The Beginning

My earliest years are tinged with shades of grey. Rain. Smoke. Sadness. My mother was a child of seventeen, fallen pregnant to a drunken criminal who was nearly thirty years old. He was abusive, and after an especially vicious beating, she returned home for help, eight months pregnant.

She battled a heroin addiction and was therefore unable to care for either of us. Eventually she left me with her family. I was often left in the care of my ten-year-old uncle, himself a bewildered child. It was my hours-long cries that prompted a neighbour to call social services. I was taken away and placed into an orphanage, from where I would eventually be fostered by two humans of pure evil.

Despite these circumstances, I always hoped that someday my mum might swoop in to rescue me. She could be the superwoman, overcomer of substance abuse, the hero that I needed throughout all of those years in hell. With foster parents who were intent on hurting me, teachers who could be bought and neighbours who chose not to see.

The story isn't over, but now I know that my mother isn't the hero. Perhaps, the hero is me.

# The Foster Home

When I was four, two adults pulled up to the kerb of the Easten European group home where I had spent the first years of my life, and with little talk I was handed over as a foster daughter. There were no cosy introductions, or a sense of Mummy and Daddy coming to save the day. I was simply placed into the backseat of a small car and driven to my new home. I was introduced to their circle of friends, which felt a bit like "Mummy and Daddy" were showing off.

However, it wasn't long before things began to change. "Here is a mop and a bucket. You need to clean this house. If you expect to live here then you are going to have to work," Mummy said.

I didn't want to call them Mummy and Daddy, and I didn't know how to clean a house, but I could tell that it was best to do as I was told.

My best wasn't good enough. After the cleaning, Mummy and Daddy would evaluate my work, and when I failed the inspection I would be made to start all over again. Sweeping, mopping, dusting, dishes, gardening for their flower market. It was exhausting, for there was always plenty of work to be done and I was merely a child.

My first physical punishment came as a result of a dropped dish slipping from my soapy little hands. The crash of broken glass was followed by the loud smack of Mummy's hand across the back of my head. I was in shock and frozen in fear. I resolved to try harder to get things right, but the beatings quickly escalated.

A smack with a belt, a stick or a hand became a daily punishment. I would clean and reclean the house, spend hours weeding or gardening for their floral business, but never to their satisfaction. Home was not safe. There was no love. I don't think they were really capable of loving me. I think they were looking for someone to work. Someone to control.

As a child as young as six I would be pulled from school to spend twelve-hour days selling flowers at the market. Though I was a young girl I had the responsibilities of an adult, and I could never meet their expectations. I doubt that they ever wanted me to. Surely they must have felt some sort of sick power as they abused me.

"I'm lucky your hair is so long, so I have something to hold onto," I was told, whipped from side to side like a rag doll, my long auburn ponytail wrapped around the hand of my foster mum. Hair pulling was a favourite way for Mummy to punish me. She could hurt me and keep me close as she hurled insults at me. I was nothing. I came from a mother who was nothing. She was crazy, and I would be too. She was an addict, and I would be too. She was a whore, and I would be too.

There was always another punishment for one of my perceived failures. If the house wasn't clean enough, if I had arrived home five minutes past my expected arrival, if my school report was less than satisfactory. In their home, there was always a reason that I deserved to be beaten.

With shame, I struggled with bed-wetting. I slept fitfully, staving off terrible nightmares. "You're too lazy to get up and use the bathroom!" she would scream, sometimes rubbing my face in the urine-soaked couch, like a puppy that was being potty-trained. I slept on a plastic sheet on the couch, making sure to empty my bladder before bed, but the habit haunted me. I would wake and feel the wet – fear setting in. If there was time I would try to clean up before they woke, but when I saw her face I knew that she hated me and that I would be beaten again.

The issues continued outside of home as well. Mummy and Daddy controlled how I dressed and how I wore my hair. I was teased by the children at school for how I looked and, cruelly, for my circumstances. A teacher had let it slip that I was living with foster parents, and I wasn't met with sympathy from my peers, but derision. Most six-year-olds dream of being a ballerina, with thoughts of candy and unicorns playing in their heads. My only thoughts were to get away. Someday I would get away.

Around age seven I fought back for the first time, arguing for the rights that I surely must have as a human. They mocked me and put me on the street. "Leave here and never come back!" Mummy screamed. It was mid-January, freezing cold as I wandered away, determined to never return. I found an unlocked door to an old apartment building, riding the lift to the eleventh floor, where I hoped no one lived. Hungry and cold, I curled on the floor to survive the night.

The walls were thin, and with each ring of the lift or unlocking of a door I jumped in fear. Surely someone was coming to take me away. In the middle of the night, I found a door leading to a rooftop. The world was asleep, the cold swirling around me. I knew that past the lights people were sleeping soundly in bed. What were they dreaming of? When had I last dreamed? I neared the edge and peered over the side. What if I just jumped? They could no longer hurt me. I wouldn't feel any pain. I could rest. What if I jumped? I was mesmerised considering the ramifications of this idea. I stood near the edge for hours.

The rising of the sun surprised me. A new day was dawning, but what would it be like for me? The realisation that the world was waking urged me to leave the safety of the building before I could be discovered. I was hungry and thirsty but knew that I couldn't return home.

With extreme thirst I headed to the street. I knew that I could drink the snow and warm myself up on the city bus. I rode back and forth to pass the day, growing hungrier, and switching buses to remain anonymous. When the sun began to set, I looked for an open door. In an apartment complex I found a small bowl of milk and kibble outside a door. It had been left for a cat, but I devoured it in hunger. I slept in hiding places again.

I recall walking on the street and glancing upon a family through a window, a warm glow of soft light around the table. The mother gently tucked a strand of hair behind her daughter's ear. They laughed over something I could not hear. They passed dishes to one another, heaping piles of food onto their plates. It was a picture of perfection; a dream I knew I could never realise. It had been years, but I was still no one's child.

A school friend's mum saw me as she was walking her dog and called me over to her. I knew that I would be back with my foster parents by the end of the night. The hunger battled the fear inside of my stomach. I felt weak and hopeless. My foster parents collected me from her with grace, so humbled and so grateful for her watchful eye, but I knew it was an act. Mummy and Daddy were never soft spoken with me. Upon returning home I was slapped across the face and raged at.

*How can they be so angry*, I wondered, *when they were the ones to tell me to leave?*

Life was a continuous cycle of hurt, pain and fear. How would I survive it?

# School

---  ◆  ---

Perhaps they underestimated me, assuming that I would be too afraid to talk about my homelife at school, but I was miserable, and at my breaking point I confided in a teacher and a social worker at school. I saw on TV the commercials that child abuse was wrong, and when I was about eleven or twelve years old I confronted them again. "You aren't allowed to treat me this way. I'm going to tell someone," I threatened.

"Who do you think will believe you?!" Mummy screamed. "You are nothing. Your mother was crazy and you're just like her!" This information was not new. I was often told that I was crazy and bad at my core, just like my mother who had chosen to leave me. My mother had chosen drugs over me.

"You are ungrateful for all we have done for you. You owe us for this life. For the food, the clothing, the roof over your head," Daddy added.

I considered this. Would I be believed? I knew that my life was not life as it should be, and full of too much pain, and I continued to long for rescue.

When an opportunity presented itself, I shared my life with an adult whom I hoped I could trust. I detailed the ridiculous expectations at home for me and the punishments I received. I described the verbal abuse, the physical abuse and the emotional abuse. I was not a mathematician, but my dad was. If I couldn't solve a problem I would be beaten and ridiculed, left at the table until midnight. I spent hours in corners, curled from the beatings and torn down by their words.

I was not saved. The system failed me immediately. "What are you complaining about? You have food, clothes and a roof over your head. What exactly are you missing out on?" one teacher said. My being ached for love, though I couldn't articulate it.

———————— ✦ ————————

My foster parents were manipulative, gifting my teachers with flowers and money, and presenting a very different face in public. Because my mother had suffered from drug and alcohol abuse and mental health problems, Mummy and Daddy pushed the narrative that I did as well. Everyone received a well-deserved spanking. I was simply blowing things out of proportion. I was told that I was going crazy, seen as mentally unstable, so instead of help, I was given heavy medications to control me. An antipsychotic medication, Chlorprothixene, was prescribed, and my foster parents gave it to me in the mornings and evenings. With the pills I became a zombie, shuffling from day to day.

There was a stint that I spent in a group home. I had run away, and when the police found me they began to take me back to my foster parents. I begged them not to. It seems crazy to me now that they were so terrible to me for so long, and it was just culturally accepted. Kids received physical punishments, it was the norm, and I "should have been grateful" to have food on the table and a roof over my head. This time I must have seemed especially desperate because instead of taking me home the police took me to a group home.

I was so much happier there. I adored the younger children, spending hours entertaining them, and I answered the social workers' questions truthfully and repeatedly. I spent about a month there, in what I hoped was time well spent. Given the choice, I told them, I would prefer to live my entire life in a group home. I had no family.

One day I was told that my foster parents were coming to take me home. "I won't see them!" I argued, but to no avail. My fate had been decided.

Seeing their faces was a knife to my heart. *How long, I wondered, until the beatings resume? How long can I last until I find the courage to run again?*

This became the new cycle. Run away, beg to not be taken home, be taken home, be beaten again, run away. No one listened to my cries for help. It had been decided that I was both mentally unstable and ungrateful. It seemed like I would be with them forever.

# Escape Attempt Number One

When I was twelve I made the decision to die. I had received an especially bad mark at school and I knew I was going to receive a severe beating. I'm not sure why that day was any different from the others. I guess I was just at my breaking point – feeling like I couldn't take it anymore.

When school let out, I went to the home of a classmate whose mum worked late hours. Of course I wasn't allowed to do this, but I knew that I couldn't face my foster parents. When darkness began to fall my foster dad arrived at the door and dragged me out by my neck. He maintained his grip as we walked home. I knew that a beating was coming, and I knew that I just couldn't take it.

He had just closed the door behind us when the doorbell rang, someone coming to buy flowers. "Stay here, we'll deal with you in a minute," he said, and he went out to help his customer. In the room my eyes searched frantically for a way to escape, landing on the bottle of pills that I had been prescribed. I remembered a movie that I had seen on TV where a young girl took too many pills and died, and instantly my mind was made up.

My nervous fingers worked to remove the childproof lid and I rushed for a glass of water to help me swallow them down. Adrenaline kicked in and I swallowed them one by one until the bottle was empty. I felt as if my decision was justified, this was no life that I was living, and I needed an escape from the pain.

I sat on the sofa, curling my legs underneath me. I could hear them chatting and laughing with their customer outside the window. My hands and feet began to go numb, my head was spinning, and as I heard a dog bark in the distance I laid my head on the pillow and closed my eyes. I felt happy and calmer than I ever had in my life.

Through a fog I heard voices, and felt the movement of my body, but the fog was too dense for me to wake. I was at peace at last.

———————— ✦ ————————

I awoke in a dimly lit room, the sight of treetops slightly moving outside the window, a soft rain tapping against the panes. A soft hand touched me. "Welcome back," she said. In confusion I thought I was with my mum, the saviour I had prayed for. Surely I had died, and my mum was there for me. I looked to her face, a blurred vision in white, unaware that it was a nurse at my bedside. *So this is what angels look like*, I thought.

When I began to realise where I was, I felt a compelling urge to run, but the gentle nurse calmed me. "You need to rest," she said. "You've been here for a few days, and you need to rest yourself." I fell back to sleep with the nurse calming me with soothing touches on my arm.

When I woke again Mummy and Daddy had arrived and when they saw that I was awake they began to yell. "Do you know how much you've embarrassed us in front of the neighbours?"

"Do you know how much business we have lost because of you?"

I was silent. How do you respond when you've just tried to end your life and your parents' only concern is the embarrassment that you've caused them? I began to cry and was overheard by the nurses nearby. One of the nurses rushed in, ushering them from my room. I cried myself back to sleep.

---

When my foster parents returned to the hospital they had large bunches of flowers for the staff, kind words of praise for the doctors and nurses who had taken care of their troubled daughter. My heart sank, knowing that they would fool the hospital staff, as they had fooled teachers and social workers. There were whispered conversations of payment. It was not uncommon for people in authority to be bribed by people with money. I was given a test to see if I was schizophrenic, and since that wasn't the case, it was decided that I'd simply been a rebellious teenager and I went home with my foster parents again.

I was back in hell.

# My Mum

By some miracle I came upon the phone number for my birth mum. There had recently been a court case where she officially lost all parental rights to me, but my treasure was in that number. I contacted her, and we made arrangements to meet up for the day. She was only a train ride away.

I knew not to ask my foster parents for permission. Though they didn't know her personally, it was clear that they hated my mum, referring to her as a bitch or a slut. I knew there would be hell to pay for seeing her, but I didn't care. Nothing could have stopped me from trying to spend time with my mum, the one I had dreamed about. It would all be worth it to wrap my arms around her once.

On that day my foster parents and I had an appointment with our social worker, Diana. I was to come straight home from school for our appointment, but instead I went to the train station. My heart was soaring, but my mind was racing. *What if she doesn't like me? What if I say something stupid and she never wants to see me again?* I breathed deeply, wondering what we would talk about. I also began to dream the dreams of my childhood. *Maybe we can run away together. Maybe we can live a simple and happy life together.*

I saw her when I got off the train. We shared a face. Could we share a life? "Hi, Mum," I said shyly.

"I hardly think I deserve to be called that," she said. We began walking towards the city centre, making awkward conversations about school and life. I was careful not to push her too much, afraid that she would be freaked out and run away from me.

Eventually my need spilled from me. "Why can't I be with you?" I asked. She stared at the ground silently, so I continued. "I really need you in my life. My foster parents are truly horrible people. I don't care where we live or what our life is like. It will be a hundred times better to be with you."

Her voice was shaking when she finally replied, "I can't care for you, Esther. I can't care for myself. I have no job. I have no home. I am so sorry that I've had to leave you, but I think your life is better without me."

I didn't argue; I could tell that it would be fruitless. She was there with me, but in her eyes she was far away. She saw the sadness on my face. "Let's have tea," she said. We walked to a cafe, and she pulled a cigarette out as we waited for service. It was silent, a heavy sadness from both of us in the air. It was a silent tea. Afterwards she walked me to the shops and encouraged me to try on a beautiful white outfit; shorts and a matching top. I emerged from the dressing room and she smiled a real and true smile.

"You look just like the old me," she said. "Let me get these for you."

I was over the moon. I had never owned anything so lovely. I had never been complimented by a parent before. I kept the new clothes on, crumpling my school uniform up into the sales bag. I felt deeply happy.

We wandered for a bit more, looking in shop windows and talking a bit. "I've got to catch the next train, Esther," she said suddenly. I flinched as if hit. "Do you smoke?" she asked.

I told the truth. "Yes," I explained. "It helps me feel a bit less stressed. Everyone at school is doing it." She bought a package of cigarettes from the shop at the train station and passed them to me. We hugged briefly, and then she was gone. I felt like I was in a puddle of grief and regret, and the fear of returning back home set in.

I sat on a bench smoking the cigarettes that she had purchased for me, aching with longing for her, and steeling myself for the onslaught that I would meet when I got back home. Though we were apart again, that day meant something to me, and I would never regret having gone to see her, regardless of the punishment that was waiting for me.

# The Last Fight

———— ✦ ————

They were upon me like wild animals when I walked through the door. Angry red faces screamed insults. "Who do you think you are? How dare you miss your appointment and embarrass us again!" She came at me with her hands instantly. She slapped me twice and then pulled back, noticing my beautiful white outfit.

"What the hell is this? Have you stolen this?" she accused. I saw her face reaching new levels of anger that I hadn't seen before, but I felt strong, rising to my full height.

"They're from my mum!" I shouted. "My mum! The one you always slag off. She loves me and she cares for me. She came to see me and it was wonderful!" I screamed, my volume matching hers.

Her eyes popped from their sockets and she turned to my foster dad. "Do you hear what this stupid cow is saying? Are you hearing this? She snuck out to see her stupid slut of a mother!" Her eyes were moving quickly. She lunged towards me, ripping my new shirt, her screams frantic as she grabbed my hair and dragged me towards the kitchen. "I'm going to teach you some respect. I should have killed you when I had a chance!" I saw stars as my head banged on the tile floor. She released me briefly and I jumped up to run, trying to get behind a closed door.

My dad pounced and dragged me back into the room, towards her. I wriggled free and ran to the china cabinet, screaming, "Don't touch me! If you touch me again I'll throw your precious china to the floor!"

A weird smile contorted his face as he turned to my mum and said, "Well look who suddenly got some nerve." He reached towards the china cabinet himself and removed a plate. Without warning he smashed it over my head. Then he grabbed me from behind and smashed my head into the doorframe. I felt blood on my head and mouth as I slumped down thinking *I got to see my mother. This is all worth it.*

"Let me go. Let me go. Let me go," I repeated. She cackled behind me like a witch.

"Where do you think you can go? Look at you. You are a wicked girl. No one will ever believe you." I jumped and ran blindly as soon as I felt her hands off me. With a burst of adrenaline I ran towards an open window and jumped through it. I felt them behind me, the wind of the devil, but I was faster. I jumped over the gate and ran into the street, my white clothes bloodied. I felt a ringing in my ears as I literally ran for my life, not slowing down until I was exhausted and could run no further.

I slumped down to breathe. I looked at what a mess I was, no plan in my mind, feeling only relief that they hadn't caught up to me yet. "Esther?" I heard a voice behind me. I turned to see a classmate from school

exiting a shop. "Oh my gosh, Esther, what happened?"
she asked. I shook my head, unsure what to say. She
put her arm around my shoulder. "Come with me," she
said. I followed her, as it was the opposite direction
from home.

She took me to her mum. I did my best to explain what
had happened and she agreed to let me stay the night.
I don't know if she believed me or not – people usually
didn't – but it was clear to see that something terrible
had happened to me. She brought me clean clothes
and a blanket for the couch. "You won't be able to stay
past tomorrow," she said, "but I can help you contact
someone for help."

I slept peacefully, with dreams of my mother in my
head. I felt confident that I wouldn't have to return to
their hell again.

# A New Family

After that day, I ended back up in a care home at the age of fifteen. Though my chances of being adopted or fostered were extremely small, I much preferred life there to being abused on a daily basis. I could live in the home until I was eighteen, and then I would be an adult in the world.

It hurt to see the younger children being taken away by smiling parents who plucked them out like kittens, but overall I was happy there. I climbed trees, played outside in the rain and played hide-and-go seek, being a child for the first time. The workers were kind to me. They knew that most children in my position would end up in a difficult life: gangs, drugs, alcohol – all were known to beckon to kids like me. It was suggested that maybe I should have stayed with my foster parents, but I knew I had made the right decision. At sixteen I would be transferred to a home for teens, and at eighteen I would be on my own.

One day I was chatting online with Sandra, a girl I had met on a past stay while I was in a mental hospital, and I opened up to her about where I was and how I came to be there. I wanted someone to know and see me. Someone to believe me. My heart longed for connection. We talked a ton over the week, and I told her everything from my life. Somehow, she convinced her mother to foster me. I didn't know it then, but money is often a motivation for foster families.

Sandra's family was struggling to make ends meet, and her mum could use the financial help for fostering a child. A few days later a smiley, chatty lady pulled into the care home car park, and after a few signatures we were off into the unknown.

We drove about three hours into a tiny village. The large sign welcoming people to town was topped with a large clock, and I clearly remember that we arrived at 7:30 pm. *My foster parents will never be able to find me here*, I thought to myself. Joana, Sandra's mum, pulled up to the kerb of a house that was half-built. "Welcome home," she said with a smile.

# Dysfunction

My new family was a mess. Joana and Tomas, the mum and dad, lived in separate rooms. Somewhere along the way, Tomas had decided to stay with his family but embrace an openly gay lifestyle. He would often be gone for work in the city, and when he was home he spent a lot of time looking for his next love online. He would close the screen immediately when one of us entered the room. He was possessive about what was his, hanging signs on the fridge such as "Don't touch my cheese!"

Joana struggled to care for her three children, and though the money they got for me helped, it was clear that I was not the priority. No one received much in the way of food or clothes, but her own children received a bit more. She worked long hours at a museum, and we kids were given free reign to care for ourselves. It was wild living there; we could do as we pleased, and had to scrounge up our own meals. Sandra and I got along all right, but she wasn't the bosom buddy I had hoped for. She clearly had her own problems, so we didn't spend much time together once I was living in her home.

The freedom I was given, mixed with my depression, was a recipe for disaster. I started at a new school but lost interest in the things that used to bring me joy. I began to skip school.

When I did attend school, I didn't fit in. I loved things that the other students did not, such as poetry. The other students expected to continue to live grey lives, working in factories when they were adults, but I didn't want to do that. I also didn't have the social skills that it took to make friends. I took on the role of class clown, but it didn't bring people closer to me. Skipping school, I would go out to the fields and listen to music or take a nap in the sun. I had a lot of time to think. I had travelled many hours, but I was still alone. No one's child.

I slept fitfully, experiencing nightmares of my old foster parents hovering over me, screaming at me and kicking me. When I woke, I would be in a sweat, depression heavy on my chest. Some days I didn't want to go to school. Some days I didn't want to leave the house, so I would lie and say that classes were cancelled. Joana either believed me or didn't care enough to press the situation.

My thoughts were consumed by the idea of purpose. *Why was I here? Why was I on Earth if no one wanted me or loved me?* My life was one merely of sadness, until I finally made a friend.

# Love

––––– ✦ –––––

Carmen was my first real friend. We met in class. Forming a friendship with her didn't feel awkward. We talked naturally as we walked down the hallways. We shared dreams and laughed over boys as we shared lunch or a cigarette. I wasn't the odd man out anymore. We were real friends.

When I woke up each morning I was no longer under a fog, and I didn't think about skipping school because I was excited to see her. She never judged me for my stories; she really got me. She shared stories about herself and her family, and the kinds of things she hoped to do one day. Carmen ignited a little fire in me that gave me a reason to live. I began smiling to myself, looking forward to each day.

One day at school we were laughing together over lunch and she pushed her hair behind her ear. It was like a slow-motion movie scene; the sun shining down and landing only on her, like a spotlight. It came as a shock when I realised that I loved her. I gasped out loud with shame. Would she see the love on my face? I turned away immediately and made an excuse to go to the bathroom. I splashed my face with cold water to wash away the feeling that surely must have been displayed on my face. I loved Carmen, but of course she couldn't know that. It did not occur to me ever that I could tell her how I felt. Being gay was considered both a massive sin before God and a mental illness. I had read online where people compared homosexuals to paedophiles, saying that people like me should be killed or thrown into prison, never again to see the light of day. This broke my heart, which had only just begun to feel happy for the first time. I had no real relationship with anyone in my foster family, I only had Carmen – and I knew I couldn't tell her. I was scared for my safety and suffering from a broken heart. My love and grief lingered in a feeling that I can't quite explain. I had only barely been given a reason to live, and now it seemed that I would be tormented in a new way.

This first love changed me. What had once given me joy now caused me pain. To be so near to her but to be quiet about my true feelings was near impossible. I felt like I was drowning.

———— ✦ ————

It wasn't long after I realised that I loved her that I did drugs for the first time. Because of my mother and my history, I had always been afraid to try them, but pain will make you do crazy things.

I was at a school party with Carmen, and kids were drinking and smoking. Kristina, a girl from school, said that she had ketamine and asked me if I wanted some. I remembered my old foster parents calling me names and saying that I would become a druggie, but I shook them from my head. "What will it feel like?" I asked.

Kristina laughed. "You won't feel. That's the point. You don't feel anything at all. You'll just have a strange sense of satisfaction." That sounded good to me – to be fulfilled for the very first time. She chopped up the amphetamines, forming it into straight white lines on the table. The world went into slow motion. *I just don't want to feel anymore*, I thought. I saw her roll up a bank note and use it to snort the drug. In moments, the first white line was gone and she was laughing, holding the bank note out to me. Fuelled by fear and adrenaline, a stupid child of seventeen, I reached for it, lowered my head and entered a whole new world.

After I snorted the line, I lay back on the couch, smoking a cigarette as I waited for the drug to take effect. My heart slowed down and my body began to tingle. I felt like I was floating and using a whole new part of my brain. There was music in the background, and I moved slowly, a smile on my face. My heart felt light. I finally had an escape. I knew I was in trouble, but I was not sure that there was anything I could do about it – or if I even wanted to.

# Life Is a Blur

The next year of my life is a bit of a blur. I did a lot of drugs and drank a lot. I was still depressed over Carmen, but the drugs suppressed my sadness. I laughed when we were together, though I longed to reach out and touch her. I saw kids at parties who were kissing and I wondered what it would be like to be with Carmen that way.

It was a regular school day when my heart got ripped out. I was sitting in class when Carmen slid into the desk next to me, a massive smile on her face. "What are you so happy about?" I asked, returning her smile.

"Roman asked me out," she answered, biting her lip. "And I said yes!" I know that my face changed instantly because it felt like a knife was being plunged into my heart. "What's the matter?" she asked. "Are you OK?" My hope that she harboured the same secret feelings had been in vain. She now had a boyfriend.

"I just have a bit of a stomach ache," I lied. I got up from my seat to approach the teacher. "May I please go to the toilet? I don't feel so good," I said.

"Sure, Esther," he answered. I felt Carmen's eyes boring into the back of my head as I made my way to the exit. I could not look at her; I was afraid that my face would give me away. I walked right out the front gates of the school and kept on walking to the edge of the village, where there was a shady little liquor store. By now I was both sad and seething in anger. I grabbed a bottle of vodka and a pack of cigarettes and placed them on the counter. The woman behind the counter asked no questions. Without being of age or possessing proper ID, I walked out of the store with my goods and continued on into the woods.

I sat on a rock sobbing, smoking and drinking from the bottle, passing the end of the school day and watching as the sun sank lower in the sky. For hours I sat, knowing that no one was coming for me, feeling that no one in the world cared for me, and knowing that I couldn't survive heartbreak again. My mind was in a spiral, every moment of darkness swirling around me and pulling me lower.

When I finished the vodka I screamed and hurled the bottle in rage. The glass shattered and I felt satisfied with the crushing sound. A piece of broken glass caught the light of the sun and glimmered; seeming like a beacon calling my name. I was manic, laughing and slapping myself across the face. "No wonder no one loves you, you are pathetic," I said aloud to myself. I got up and reached for the largest piece of glass, a yearning to pull it across my skin. I knew that cutting yourself was not something that a "normal" happy person would do, but I had a compulsion to do so. I had to know how it would feel. I pushed the glass against my wrist and quickly dragged it horizontally.

A sharp pain broke through my fog, a bright red forming on my arm. It was such a contrast to the drab grey sky. While I watched the blood flow, it was another release for me. I sat in the woods until it was dark and then made my way home in the shadows. It was night and the doors were locked, so I went through my bedroom window, no one having noticed that I hadn't been home all along.

———— ✦ ————

The year continued to pass in a blur of alcohol. I could barely stand to see Carmen, it was hard to be excited for her and Roman, and I started skipping school more and more. I was failing nearly everything. I played the class clown when at parties in an attempt to mask how I was really feeling. People laughed with me, or at me, but I kept everyone at a distance. I wasn't truly known anymore; not even superficially as I had been with Carmen.

When I could no longer bear to see Carmen, I made the decision to leave the village and go to a boarding school. At nearly eighteen, I was free to make that decision. I packed my bags and moved to a new school in a different town before Christmas. In the new school, my dormitory room was freezing; it was nearly minus-fifteen degrees. A thin cracked window and rotting wood frame let in more than they were keeping out, so I put on every jumper I owned to fight the cold. I had a roommate, but she was never there. I was starving, so I picked the lock on her cabinet to steal a few lasagne noodles. Since it was Christmas time, most people were home for the holidays, so it was as if I was alone in the dorms. I would wander the halls, occasionally switching on the communal TV with three channels, but eventually I was desperate for food. There was a girl that I knew from my old school who lived in the dorm as well, and I knocked on her door to beg. I couldn't meet her eyes, and she seemed confused at first, but she let me in and gave me all of her canned goods. I accepted them greedily, like a kid in a candy store, but my hunger kept me from being proud.

The next day her mother was there and they knocked on my door. They sat on my bed and began to ask me questions. "Where is your family?" she asked.

"I haven't got any," I told her. I explained that I was on my own, giving a brief synopsis of my history.

"Where are you getting your money from?" she asked.

"I haven't got any," I said. Neither set of foster parents had ever given me any of the money they were given for caring for me. She looked at me with pity and I realised that I had been naive. Of course they had received money for me, but they had kept it all for themselves.

She wrote down an address. "Go here. They will help you," she said. I bundled up and headed into the cold. I walked about four miles to the address on the paper, where I was given two heavy bags full of food. I was so happy. The woman there gave me another address and told me to go there the next day. They would help me sign up for government assistance. I would no longer starve. Though the bags were heavy and the walk was long and cold, I was bursting with happiness. The next day a classmate's mum was the employee at the government facility who helped me sort out my paperwork. She advised me on how to get a bankcard. I was embarrassed to be seen as being this desperate, but I felt so grown up signing up for a bankcard.

A month later I began receiving a monthly cheque. There was relief in that, but I was a disaster with budgeting. I had no experience with money – saving or planning. I had no adult in my life to teach me, so I quickly began to waste it. Though I wasn't using drugs anymore, I bought alcohol and cigarettes. The access to alcohol brought a new set of friends around me, who took advantage of what I could provide them. I was rarely alone, but I was never happy. It was better than my life with my foster parents and better than pining away for Carmen, but I still felt so alone.

# Sonia

Sonia was a new girl at school. She was tall, blonde and lovely, but she carried herself a little roughly – tracksuits and a scowl. I admired her vibe. She was a diamond in the rough. Though she carried herself with confidence, I recognised something broken behind her eyes. No one would mess with her. We didn't become friends immediately, but we saw each other at parties, and after a few drunken conversations we began to form something deeper. I know that she could see that I was broken as well.

"So what's your story?" she asked, flicking the ash from a cigarette.

"What do you mean?" I asked.

"Who are you, Esther? Where do you come from?" she asked.

I guess my tongue was loosened by the vodka, and I started to share a bit about my past. I told her about the beatings and my suicide attempt. She grabbed my hand when I described having never been loved. "Me too," she said. She told me about her absent father, alcoholic mother, and the way she had always felt alone. We told each other all of our worst stories, finding comfort in our commonalities.

After that we were pretty much inseparable. When we weren't together physically, we were checking on each other by phone. Once when my roommate was away, Sonia came over to stay the night, even though it was against the rules. We were chatting and listening to music when she casually pulled a bag of drugs from her pocket. "I'm sorry, Esther, but I need to let you know that I've been using drugs," she said tentatively. She looked scared to see my reaction.

I rushed to reassure her. "It's OK," I said. "I've done drugs before too. It's all right with me." She looked relieved, asking for permission with her eyes. She began to make a line for herself, bending down to snort away her pain. Though she was the one using, I felt the rush, remembering how it felt to be high, and I gently took the bill from her hand. She laughed softly as I bent down to snort the next line.

We collapsed back onto the bed, quiet as the drugs kicked in. We stayed up all night, chatting about anything and everything. She took my hand in hers and my heart felt full. I had finally found a companion. I wondered if she was like me, finding an attraction to other girls, or if she was feeling like a sister to me. I didn't want to find out, so I kept my questions to myself.

———————— ✦ ————————

Later that week another girl at school said something mean about me, and when I told Sonia about it she was furious. She rushed across the campus to confront the girl and defend me. The girl quickly apologised; Sonia could be scary. My mind was blown. After years of being picked on, I finally had someone to stand up for me. My devotion was sealed. I was like a puppy following her around. I was relieved not to be alone. We continued to spend most of our time together, though more and more often we were high.

After some time Sonia's moods began to change. I knew it was the drugs. Addictions make you crazy. She was full of laughter and connection to me if we were using, but she would push me away in anger if we didn't have drugs. I did what I could to make her happy, spending all of my money on drugs. I pawned my phone when I got desperate to get us high and I was out of money. I knew that she had a boyfriend who was also giving her drugs, but I had never met him. I wanted her to like me best. When she was with him I was miserable, so I would buy more drugs to share with her and she would come back around. When we were high, it was as if we had never been apart – another toxic cycle in my life.

She did just enough to keep me devoted, holding my hand, complimenting me, listening to me when I was sad. One night she kissed me gently. I felt my insides warm as she said, "You mean so much to me, Esther. I can't imagine my life without you." The thought of her boyfriend popped into my mind, but I pushed that away. Her kiss gave me hope that I would never be alone.

I remember one night that we drove out to the forest. We had a bag full of drugs and our favourite playlist.

We stayed there all night, getting high and devoting ourselves to one another under the stars and the trees. She held my hand. "I am so relieved that we found each other," she said. I fell deeper and deeper into my devotion to her.

Looking back I can see that Sonia was just as addictive for me as the ketamine. She made me feel loved and accepted, both as part of a family and as a companion. I needed her.

When she would pull away to be with her boyfriend it would destroy me, but I didn't run away like I did with Carmen. With Sonia I tried harder to earn her love. I was simultaneously happy and miserable.

Once she went quiet for a week, staying away and ignoring my calls and messages. I knew she was with her boyfriend and I was devastated. I drank and used heavily to cope with the emotions that were overwhelming me.

I was drunk for two days straight when something snapped inside of me. My roommate was away and I was so angry that Sonia was ignoring me. It felt like my soul was lit on fire and, in a rage, I began to smash everything in my room. I threw things to the floor, growing in anger as glass shattered around me. I screamed out, turning my room into a storm. I grabbed a shard of glass from the floor and dragged it across my arm, remembering the sweet release of letting the pain out this way. I slashed myself several times, gradually relaxing into a less manic state. I opened the door, smearing blood across the surface, to go and smoke in the designated area. I didn't care what I looked like. I saw lots of students staring or laughing. "She's really gone crazy, hasn't she?" a girl whispered loudly to her friend. I sat on the edge of the couch, blood across my arms and inhaled deeply. *No one cares about you. No one loves you, and if you were dead, no one would miss you.* I finished the cigarette and went to my room to send a text to my dealer.

"Can you sell me a gun?"

I found out that evening how easy it is to get a gun. He replied, "Yes". I went to the ATM, and a few minutes later I was walking back to my student accommodation with a handgun in a paper bag. I would finally end this.

# Russian Roulette

———— ✦ ————

Back in my room I settled onto my bed with the gun, three bullets and an almost empty bottle of vodka. I listened to another sad song play and made up my mind, loading the bullets into the gun.

I took a long swig of vodka and closed my eyes, inserting the barrel of the gun into my mouth. In the darkness I saw my foster mum holding me down. She whipped me and screamed how much she hated me. "You're nothing but a crazy drunk, just like your whore of a mum. You'll never be anything," she screamed. I pulled the trigger.

CLICK.

I laughed manically. The vodka and the adrenaline had turned me into a fool. I took another swig from the bottle and put the gun to my temple. I closed my eyes. In the darkness I saw Carmen watching me as I ran from the classroom. I saw the face of Sonia, lying across from me, gently running her thumb across my hand. Where was she now? I pulled the trigger a second time.

CLICK.

I was incredulous. I reached again for the bottle, but it was empty, so I reached across the bed for my pack of cigarettes. The gun was teetering on the edge and I accidentally pushed it over the edge. It clattered onto the floor and fired.

BAAAM!

The noise was deafening. The bullet ricocheted off the door and I erupted into a mad fit of laughter. Within moments I heard a loud knock at the door and my mind began to race. I had to hide the gun. I shoved it into the closet. Outside my door I heard the security woman yelling, "What the hell is going on in there?"

"Nothing," I yelled back through the door.

"I've called the police. They're really going to sort you out this time!" she yelled. I panicked, grabbing my phone. I pulled on a jacket, shoved a few belongings into a backpack, opened the door, and used all of my might to push past security and down the hall. I reached the stairway and continued running. The stairs felt never-ending, but as I reached the end I saw that I had beaten the police and no one was waiting for me there. I rushed out into the cold, calling the only person I could think of. Miraculously, she answered.

"I'm in trouble. Please come and get me?" I asked.

She must have heard the absolute dread and panic in my voice. "I'll be there in two minutes," Sonia answered. I hid behind a tree until I saw her car take the corner. She always drove like a race car driver. I ran from behind the trees and darted into the passenger seat. Instantly we were off, speeding through the night to safety.

I held my breath. *What will happen to me now? Where will I go?*

I would never return to school again.

# Hiding Out

We drove through the city streets as darkness fell. She pulled up to the kerb at her friend Monica's apartment. I didn't know Monica well, but I had met her a handful of times when she had attended parties with Sonia. She was a single mum, and she wasn't happy about it. I had never found her pleasant, but if she was willing to give me a place to stay, I was grateful.

Sonia walked with me up ten flights of stairs to Monica's sour studio apartment. The odour was strong as the door swung open and Monica stood, dark and serious eyes, with a crying toddler on the floor behind her. It smelled like smoke, mould and urine, drenched in the scent of a cheap perfume that was failing to conceal the stench.

"I can't stay here with you, Esther," said Sonia. "I have some business to take care of, but you know I'll be back." I nodded a silent understanding, following Monica to a droopy couch.

Monica attempted to pacify her daughter, and when she was settled turned to me.

"What happened?" she asked in a thick Russian accent.

I shook my head, unable to answer. "Come with me," she said. There was a tiny washroom where she lit two cigarettes. Her daughter's small pink clothes were hung to dry in our swirling smoke. I pieced together a brief story of the gun and my game, Monica's dark eyes boring into me as she continued to ask questions.

We went back to the couch, where I stared at a TV and Monica busily texted on her phone. I was empty. It would be hours before I allowed myself to sleep.

———— ✦ ————

When I woke up, the sun was just coming in through the window and I could hear Monica on the telephone. I couldn't make out the words, but her tone was hushed and secretive. It didn't even take a second for me to fill up with dread. I remembered the night before. When the baby woke, Monica dressed her and headed to the door. "I'll be home in just a minute. I'm taking Irina to the day-care." I nodded, having no real words. *Where is Sonia?* My phone had died and Monica's charger didn't match it.

I sat in silence while she was gone, staring out the window at the cold street below.

When Monica returned I spoke up. "When is Sonia coming back? Do you know? I haven't heard from her and I need to know what's going on."

"It's too early to call her," said Monica. "Let's eat breakfast and then see what she says."

I nodded. Without a phone, the calls were not my own to make. She boiled the kettle and made an egg and toast, but I was too nervous to manage anything. *What is going on in the outside world?*

After eating, Monica put the phone to her ear and left the room. She came back with a serious look. "I called Sonia, but there was no answer," she said. We passed the morning in silence; Monica watching TV and smoking, me smoking and worrying. It was after lunch when her phone rang. Her eyes narrowed and grew dark, gasping when she read the message on her screen. She looked shocked.

"What is it?" I asked.

"It's a message from Sonia, and it's not good news," she said. "The police have checked your dorm room and they found your gun. The cops are all over your school, questioning people about where you are."

I could barely manage an "Oh no!" before she continued.

"You need to stay here. It's not safe for you to go out." I nodded in understanding, turning my useless phone over and over in my hands. "We need to get rid of your phone as well. Take out the SIM card and we will throw it all in the bin. We don't want the police to track you using that." I nodded again, following instructions.

"When is Sonia coming?" I asked.

"It isn't safe. Everyone at school knows that you two are friends. The cops might follow her here. We need to have you lay low for a while." I barely moved throughout the whole afternoon, wondering about what would happen to me. *What are the police going to do to me when they find me? How can I get out of this? I wish I had killed myself when I had the chance.*

Eventually Monica left to pick Irina up from day-care, and I took a shower, trying to wash the darkness away. When Monica returned she had a bottle of vodka to share with me. "Maybe this will help calm your nerves," she said, pouring me a cup. Grateful, I gulped. On an empty stomach, I was drunk quickly.

"Where are your parents?" she asked.

"I haven't got any," I answered.

"Don't worry, Esther. I don't mind you staying here for a few days while you figure things out." She offered her first smile.

"Thank you," I said, taking another large swallow. "Do you think I can use your phone to talk to Sonia?"

"She said she couldn't talk tonight," Monica answered quickly. She smoked cigarettes through the evening, laughing at some programme on the TV that I couldn't even hear. Thanks to the vodka I was able to sleep, but it was restless. I couldn't see a way out of this situation.

Monica woke me in the morning with a cup of strong coffee. A bowl of porridge was steaming at the table. "Have some breakfast," she said. She watched with her dark eyes as I ate. Eventually she asked, "Have you figured out what you are going to do?"

I shook my head vigorously. "No," I said. "I don't have a clue." I broke down in tears, sobbing at the table. She picked up her mug of coffee and walked away. I cried on the table until I was empty, but she didn't return. She took the baby to the day-care again and returned quietly.

I ate very little that day, not wanting to burden Monica any further. She spent most of her time texting, though she said there were no more messages coming from Sonia. I fell asleep very early, not waking again until the next morning when Monica returned from the day-care drop-off. "We need to sit down," she said, her face very serious.

"What's wrong?" I asked, cringing. Obviously, everything was wrong. "What did you hear?" I asked.

"I talked to Sonia. The police are still searching for you. When they find you they plan on charging you with illegal gun possession and attempted murder."

I gasped. "Murder! I didn't attempt to murder anyone!"

"Yes, but you fired the gun in your room, didn't you? That bullet could have hurt someone. It could have killed someone."

"But it didn't," I argued weakly.

"It doesn't matter to the police," she said. "You're in huge trouble, Esther. When the police catch you, you'll be arrested and put away. They are saying that you can get up to ten years in prison."

"I can't," I argued back.

"You don't want to go to prison, Esther. It's terrible there." She paused to stare at me seriously, as if I didn't already know that I wanted to avoid prison. "You have a very pretty face, and people will hurt you. Some older prisoner will claim you as their property. They'll use you and rape you. You'll have to do whatever they say."

I began to cry more deeply. I was not a murderer. I didn't want to go to prison. I would never have harmed someone. I only wanted to hurt myself and end this terrible life. When I closed my eyes, my foster parents were there, red-faced and screaming. "You are nothing but a loser, like your mum!" they raged.

"You need to figure out what to do," said Monica, leaving me on the couch to cry and pray.

*Please, God*, I pleaded. *If you are there, please help me. I would never hurt someone else. Please, God, keep me from going to prison. I want my mum, God. Please let this be another terrible nightmare. Please let me wake up in my room, all of this having been a dream. Please, God. Please. Please. Please.* In my sorrows my mum and God were intermixed, and I spent the afternoon calling out to both of them.

Hours later Monica left to get Irina again. "Please ask Sonia to call me," I begged.

"Of course, love. I've been asking her, but she doesn't think it's safe. We don't want the police to find you because of her." She offered me a weak smile.

I understood her logic but felt that seeing Sonia would help me formulate a plan. She was the only one who had been on my side.

When Monica returned, we sat at the table again, a limp salad and a glass of vodka in front of each of us. "We need to figure out a plan," she said. "The longer you wait here, the better chance of you being found by the police."

"I don't know what to do," I said.

"I once had a friend who was in trouble," she said. "She decided to go to another country. It was hard on her at first to leave Eastern Europe, but she found a good job, and is living a good life. I heard from her recently and she was happy. Do you know anyone in a different country?"

"No," said. "I hardly know anyone."

She shrugged. "Well let me ask around," she said.

"Thank you, Monica," I said. She went to the couch with her phone, texting again. I finished my drink and poured another. The vodka would help me sleep. Around midnight her phone rang aloud. She read the text and smiled.

"Good news, Esther. Sonia has an uncle who owns a hotel in London. He said that if you go there you can work in the hotel as a waitress or a cleaner, and he'll let you sleep in one of the rooms, so you'll have a place to live." She smiled a broad smile.

"Yes," I said. "I could do that." When I thought about it, it made lots of sense. I had loads of experience in cleaning and hard work, thanks to my foster parents. I *could* go to live with Sonia's uncle.

"Trust me," she said, "this is great news." I nodded.

"Will you be OK to leave Eastern Europe?" she asked, concern in her eyes.

"Yes, I can ... I've never really felt that I fit in here anyway. I have no family, and really no friends."

"Don't say that," she said. "You have Sonia. And now you have me. We will help get you to safety, but we'll need to get you on a flight right away, before the police have a chance to put you on a no-fly list."

I shook my head. "But I don't have any money," I said. "How will I purchase a ticket?"

"Don't worry," she said. "I'll buy you the ticket, and then when you get to London you can pay me back when you get your first paycheque. It's not a problem."

"Oh my gosh, that would be wonderful. Thank you," I said. I honestly couldn't believe that she was offering so much to me, but I felt relief. I could see myself in London. I could start over. I could be happy.

She texted for a few minutes and then looked up. "Get out your passport. My friends are going to come around to pick it up to go buy you a ticket."

"Oh, really," I said. Things felt like they were progressing really quickly, but they were right. The police could put me on a no-fly list, and then I'd be caught at the airport. *I can't go to prison.*

"Yes, my friends are really nice. It's so good of them to come around and help you out."

"Yes, it is," I agreed.

There was a knock on the door soon after, and two men walked in, dressed in dark clothing. Their clothing looked expensive and they were smiling.

"We're sorry to hear about your trouble, but we are happy to help you out," said the taller of the two. He offered me a smile.

"Go ahead and give me your passport," said the other. As I walked towards them, it seemed as if the first was taking my picture on their phone, but I couldn't be too sure. It seemed like an odd angle to be holding his phone, but I didn't want to question these men who had come to help me. I didn't hesitate to hand over my passport.

"We'll be back," they said, exiting as quickly as they entered.

"It's going to be OK now, Esther. This plan is going to work," said Monica. She offered me another cigarette and another vodka. We sat in companionable silence.

In less than an hour her friends returned with my passport and a ticket. "You'll be leaving first thing in the morning," the first one said.

"OK. Thanks," I said. My mind was racing. It seemed to be moving so fast, but I assured myself of what I had been told. "Thank you for your help," I said again to all of them.

Monica's dark eyes smiled as I thanked them. I wanted to ask them why they had taken my picture, but I couldn't be sure and I didn't want to seem ungrateful for the way that they were helping me, so I said nothing.

After they left I pulled my things out of my backpack. I had very little with me. My yellow Mickey Mouse hoodie was filthy and my shoes were falling apart. Monica saw this and spoke up. "You should wash up so you don't look like a bum in the airport. I'll give you one of my jackets and clean up your clothes for you."

"Thank you so much for everything," I said. In the shower I let my mind wander. *What will London look like? I can't wait to see all of the lights. I can't wait to work and earn money and make something of myself. It's all going to be OK.* My pep talk was helping me wrap my head around all of this sudden change.

When I got out of the shower Monica was waiting for me with a pair of her pyjamas, my clothes drying behind her. "I've been thinking while I washed," she said. "Since you have a past of suicide attempts, we should fake your death before you go. We can leave your student ID and some of your other items down by the river, and if the police find it all, they'll believe that you've killed yourself. Then no one will be looking for you. It's genius," she said.

It sounded strange to me, almost like a scene from a movie, but I wouldn't need my student ID anyway, and I was so tired. I passed her a bundle of belongings and she put them into a bag. I settled into sleep on the sofa with visions of London dancing in my head. I don't know if she left the house while I slept, but I assumed she did to carry out her plan.

———————◆———————

Monica woke me early, just enough time to dress in her clothing and run a brush through my hair, and then her friends from the night before were downstairs to give us a ride. I was surprised but grateful to see that Monica would be joining us at the airport.

"Don't act nervous in the airport," said the older man. "If they ask you where you're going, tell them you're going on holiday to visit your sister for a couple of weeks."

"If security sees you acting nervous they might not let you on the plane," said Monica.

That didn't make sense to me, but I nodded my agreement.

"OK," I agreed. When we arrived at the capital airport Monica walked me to the gate.

"Dalia, a friend of Sonia's uncle, will be meeting you at the airport there. I told her what you look like and what you are wearing. She has blonde hair. Just look for her and she will take you to the hotel."

"OK," I said.

"Good luck, Esther," she said, giving me a slight hug.

"Thank you for everything, Monica," I said.

"Of course," she said. I walked towards the gate in Monica's coat with a backpack full of nothing. Clutching my passport and my ticket in hand, I approached security, remembering to plaster on a smile.

"What is your purpose for travelling to London?" he asked.

"I'm going to London to visit my sister for Christmas," I said.

"You don't seem to have much stuff," he said. I hadn't expected a reply.

"My sister already has everything that I need," I said, thinking quickly.

He scanned my documents while I held my breath. "Enjoy your trip," he said. I couldn't believe it; I was on my way to freedom.

———— ✦ ————

I had never been on a plane before, but it felt amazing. I was amazed by the views from the sky, feeling like a bird let out of its cage. Adrenaline pumped through me as we flew further from the darkness of my life towards the possibility of my future. The sun was finally shining on me.

# London

---◆---

It didn't take long to fly to London. I exited the plane, eighteen and in wonder at the bustle all around me. Passengers were met by friends and family, wrapped up in hugs and kisses. I looked around for a woman who might be Dalia, but no blonde woman seemed to be looking for me.

I kept walking in the crowd, scanning the faces for someone who was looking for me, but I didn't see her anywhere. I whipped around when I felt a tap on my shoulder. A man was standing there. "Hello," he said. "I'm Tomas. I'm here to pick you up."

"I'm supposed to be meeting a woman named Dalia," I said.

"She couldn't make it, so she sent me and my mate," he said. "See?" he held his phone up to me so I could see a picture of myself.

"Oh," I said. How did he have my photo?

"We need to get out of the airport. I don't want to pay for parking," he said. "Let's go." He turned to walk through the crowd and I quickly followed after him.

I had never seen so many people in one place before. It was overwhelming, so I kept up with Tomas.

When we got to the car he introduced me to the driver, Marius. "Let's go get something to eat," Tomas said. We stopped for food right outside the airport as Tomas took a phone call. "Yeah, I got her," he said. When he hung up he said that it was Dalia checking on me. He ordered me a meal and encouraged me to sleep. "It will be at least an hour," he said. I looked out of the windows at all the lights. The signs were covered in names that I couldn't pronounce. We inched our way in the traffic of the city.

The car came to a stop on London Bridge. I couldn't believe how beautiful it was.

The city was decorated with Christmas trees and ornaments, and the lights twinkled. It was December 18th, and I was so happy to be in London, on the first day of my new life. We were in the car for a couple of hours, but my joy didn't fade.

I was surprised when we pulled up to a terraced house, and not the hotel. Tomas spoke before I did. "We are going to go to the hotel and meet up with Dalia tomorrow. We'll stay here tonight." I felt uneasy for the second time since getting off the plane, but also powerless to speak up. I couldn't demand that he take me to the hotel.

I followed Tomas and Marius up a narrow flight of stairs. As we came to the top the smell of smoke was strong, and the thumping of loud music was in the air. When he opened the door there were five men at a table, drinking and playing cards. Tomas rushed in whispering as the men turned to look at me. I was barely within the room, feeling more uncomfortable with each second that passed, as Marius locked the door behind me.

"Do you know why you're here?" Tomas asked.

"Yes," I said.

"Do you know why you're here?" he asked again, his face changing before me. Laughter followed.

"I'm here to work at my friend's uncle's hotel," I said slowly, enunciating each word as my blood turned cold.

"You'll be working alright, but I don't know about any hotel," he said, a twisted smile on his face.

"What do you mean?" I asked, beginning to panic.

His eyes went cold and dead. "Ah, you're so stupid. So young and stupid, aren't you? You're here to be my bitch. You'll do exactly as I tell you, or whatever my friends here tell you to do."

I went numb. There was nothing I could do except stand and listen to the evil coming from his mouth. I turned and saw the door behind me. There were four bolted locks and several men blocking my way out.

"You should have checked where you were going, shouldn't you? I've seen plenty of stupid little whores like you, coming to London hoping for some happy fairy tale." I took a single step towards the door. "If you try to run, I will kill you," he said. "The doors are locked and there are seven of us here. And don't bother screaming, because we have no neighbours," he said, walking closer to me. He put his hand on my chin. "You are my property now. I will do whatever I want to you, so put that in your stupid little head." He walked his fingers up to my temple and pulled them, as if they were a trigger. I flinched and his mates laughed. "Sit down," he instructed, "but pass me a beer first." His mates all laughed as I twisted in sickness. "And there's one for you as well. I'm feeling very nice today." I followed his instruction and sat on an empty chair. An icy dread came over me.

I saw the signs now: Sonia's disappearance from my life, Monica's scheme to fake my death, the photo on the man's phone. How much had they earned for me? Half of me was in shock. Half of me accepted that I had simply exchanged one level of hell for another. I closed my eyes and saw my mum. There could be no rescue now. My life would never be the same.

# Rape

Tomas had the smile of the devil. His skin was scarred from acne, his teeth were yellow and his eyes were dark, the whites just a speck. As I sat in shock and fear, he kept me close, whispering threats and boasting to his mates. "See, she's not even crying. She knows she has to be a good girl or she will end up in a ditch." He kept his hand on my shoulder. His dirty nails dug in each time that he insulted me.

The room felt like it was shrinking. The men at the table carried on drinking and laughing, turning into wolves before me. They traded bets about who would have me first. I turned slightly towards Tomas. I had to risk his response. "Please let me leave. I won't go to the police. I promise. I will just disappear."

He brought his yellow teeth closer and sneered in my face. "Why would I ever do that? I don't give a damn about you. But you're such a pretty little thing. You're going to make me lots and lots of money." His mates raised their glasses in laughter.

"Please," I begged, "I haven't slept with anyone before. I'm a virgin." I was hoping to build some sympathy with my captor, but instead it sent them into a frenzy.

"A virgin! You'll get great money for a virgin, Tomas. You seem to be winning here!" shouted one of the wolves.

Tomas wrapped his hand around my neck, an evil smile twisting his face. "The highest bidder here can take this virgin and turn her into a woman. A woman who can be turned into a good little seller and make me some money!" He slapped his leg as if he had told a great joke.

I felt small again, a little girl up against the beatings of my foster parents – I remembered that if I were compliant, they would lighten up a little. I felt it might be the same with Tomas. Fighting back would only increase his evil.

The men continued to drink, stumbling around drunkenly, but Tomas stayed fixed by my side. When I asked to use the toilet, he walked me down the hall and stood in the doorway. "Get used to it. You won't be alone for a very long time," he said. With shame I pushed down my jeans and urinated. His eyes never left me.

When his mates finally left, he arranged a pile of cushions on the floor. My stomach crawled into my throat and I prepared myself for what would happen next. "Lie there and go to sleep. Whores like you don't get a bed," he said. I felt a slight amount of relief that Tomas was not going to rape me, for now, but I lay in dread. He lay on a mattress right next to me and was quickly snoring. I had seen his gun, his knife, and the locks on the door. I was a prisoner. I couldn't sleep, waiting for the sun to come through the window.

In the morning Tomas took me by the neck and pushed me towards the kitchen. "Cook me breakfast," he ordered. I stumbled towards the fridge, removing eggs. There was a loaf of bread on the counter, so I made toast as I fried two eggs. He watched from the table. When I began to cry, he yelled, "No! You don't cry. It won't help. Just follow my orders."

I passed the plate and he swallowed everything quickly, leaving a sliver of toast on his plate. He pushed it back towards me. "There's your breakfast." I didn't move quickly enough, so he leapt across the table and shoved the bread into my mouth. "Eat, slut! Since when are you too good to eat what's left over?"

I choked down the toast and then he walked me to the shower. He stood in the bathroom and told me to shower. My body was shaking, I was so afraid. The sense of doom was growing, not only internally, but I felt physically surrounded by darkness. He watched closely as I climbed into the tub and let the water run around me. His eyes violated me. He passed me a razor.

"Shave everything. No one will want to touch you if you stay like that." Shaking, I took the razor in my hand.

Robotically I did as I was told. I was so afraid of him and what he might do to me. How much worse things could be for me if I argued or resisted.

When the shower ended I sat there on the floor. He began to take shots of vodka and make phone calls. He presented me as good news to all that he called. "Good news, mate. I have a new girl. Fresh meat. And she's a virgin!" he cackled into the phone. I curled into a ball, trying to turn off my brain and my heart.

When it was dark, Tomas pulled out a box of condoms. Soon, there was a knock on the door. "We have a guest," Tomas said. "Someone very special is coming to see you." He opened the door and a bloke walked in and straight towards me. He was nearly drooling.

"You weren't lying when you said you had a pretty little thing," he told Tomas. Tomas picked me up by the neck and walked me down the hall. He shut the door and I was alone with the man. Tears came quickly.

"Please don't do this. I haven't done this before. Please," I begged.

He took off his pants. "Get undressed. I didn't pay all that money for you to just sit there."

I cried, but he laughed, "It's OK. Soon you will know exactly what to do with a man." I trembled, and he advanced upon me, forcing his way into my body. I tried to distance myself as I was ripped with pain. My tears and my fear did nothing to stop him. He pumped until he was finished. He was smiling as he put his trousers on and left the room.

"Tomas, that money was well worth it," he shouted. I lay on the bed, feeling like death. I could smell his aftershave and feel his weight, though he was no longer in the room. I was a whore now. There was nothing I could do. I cried out to God. *Why is this happening to me? Is it because of the gun?*

When the door shut Tomas came to me in the room. "Get into the shower." He saw the blood on the bed and sneered. "Guess these sheets need to go in the bin. But at least you can start working for me now. Make me some money."

I went to the shower, but nothing could make me feel clean. I scrubbed in the hottest water I could stand. My mind remembered all the people I had known. *Is Carmen in class somewhere? What is Sonia doing right now? What would my schoolmates think if they knew what has happened to me?* I couldn't stop myself from crying, though I was afraid that it would make Tomas angrier if he heard me.

He did. "Hurry up and quit crying!" Tomas ordered. "You brought this upon yourself." From the shower, he guided me to the table and sat down next to the pile of money that the bloke had paid him. He smiled. He reached towards me, holding out a cigarette.

I sat feeling like I was going to be sick. "Take it," he screamed. I reached for the cigarette. "Congratulations. You're a woman now."

# Hell

———— ✦ ————

In the morning I made breakfast again and was given scraps to eat again. Tomas began drinking again. He made phone calls again. He smiled. He laughed. I felt dead again. I was so afraid, and hungry. I was sick.

"Make yourself presentable," he said. "My friends are on their way." My heart sank when I saw how he looked at me, like I was a pound sign in his eyes and not a girl. When his mates arrived, he grabbed me by the neck and pushed me in the room. Again.

When the door closed I was alone with a friend of Tomas's. He leered at me, lunging forward while unbuckling his trousers.

That night was hell. One by one his mates came into the room to abuse me. Not one of them saw me as a human being; to each of them I was just a toy. I pleaded for them to stop, but no one showed concern or empathy. "Cheer up. If you're crying I can't get excited," I was told by a few. That was a lie; they *could* each get excited as I cried beneath them.

I didn't feel like a woman, as Tomas had predicted; I felt like death. No matter how long it went on, it was painful and nightmarish.

I don't know how much time passed. It could have been hours or it could have been days. It was just hell. I died to myself. I sank deeper into sorrow and shame and pain because of what they were doing to me. I was let out of the room occasionally to shower or use the toilet. I hoped one of them would hold down on my neck long enough to kill me because I knew I couldn't go on like this.

# Christmas

After some days Tomas brought me to the table, passing me a cigarette. "Do you know what tomorrow is?" he asked.

"No," I answered.

"It's Christmas, and you are going to cook us a Christmas dinner. If you do a good enough job maybe you can have the night off!" This surprised me somehow. He was already using me as a slave, and now I had to make his celebratory meal too?! There were many moments when I looked at him to try to see what kind of person he really was. *Deep down, how could he be so evil? How could torturing another human come so easily to him?*

The next day he presented me with a bag of groceries. "Get on with it!" he said, shoving me into the kitchen. Tomas was never nice to me. Even when he was offering me a cigarette, it was with malice.

His friends began to arrive, one by one, looking festive and cheery. "Who's that?" they asked.

"Don't worry about her. She's just here to make us our Christmas dinner and serve us." As the drinks flowed his answers escalated. "She's here to serve us in any way that we want. She's my Christmas present to you."

He continued to degrade me, coming to the kitchen to slap me and scream in my face.

"Stop moping around and get on with dinner," he yelled. I had little cooking experience, especially with the kind of meal he was expecting, but fear helped me to figure it out.

When the meal was served I heard laughter and joy coming from the next room. The sound of plates being scraped, music and happy holiday voices. Occasionally one of them would wander into the kitchen and laugh. "Good little slave you got here, Tomas," they said with a wink. One of them brought me a paper plate with some scraps from the table. "Since it's Christmas, I'll be nice and let you have a bite to eat, but you can't eat from the same plates as me. Never know if a dirty slut like you has AIDS or something." Tomas came into the kitchen, laughing as he heard his friend degrade me. He sat next to me, set a glass down in front of me and poured a full glass of vodka.

"Drink," he ordered. I sat. "Drink. It's Christmas," he said.

"I can't drink all of that," I said.

"Drink," he screamed. He jumped up, grabbed me by the neck, and when I gasped, he poured the vodka into my throat. I choked, but plenty of it went down my throat. I sat gasping for breath as he poured another.

"More," his friend encouraged him. He grabbed me again and poured vodka down my throat. They forced me to drink at the table with them until I threw up on my feet.

"You're disgusting," Tomas said. The room began to spin, and all the voices and laughter and noises merged together as one.

---

When I woke up it was morning again. Shivering, I realised that I was naked. I could smell aftershave on my skin, piecing together what had happened to me after I passed out the night before. Though I couldn't sit up I could see bruises on my body. Everything was in pain. It was so intense that I couldn't tell where it was coming from. I passed out again.

"Wake up, you slut. You stink. Get in the shower." Tomas woke me, prodding his feet into my side, and pushed me down the hall towards the shower. My head was spinning, and as I stepped into the tub, I vomited again. I quickly washed it away, continuing to retch as I bathed myself the best I could. I was weak and in so much pain. He walked me from the shower to the table, throwing a takeaway bag at me. "Eat," he said. I slowly chewed a piece of bread, swallowing the urge to vomit. "I'm taking you out to the tanning bed. You need to get a tan. No one will want you looking so pale. You need to be presentable."

I laced my shoes and followed Tomas to the door and down the stairs. The sun and fresh air hit my skin for the first time in I don't know how many days. *Is there a chance for me to escape? Can I run? Can I let someone know that I need help? Can I knock on a window and scream for help?* Tomas was behind me as if he could read my mind. He put his hand on my neck. "Don't even think about doing anything stupid. I am faster than you, and I have a knife right here in my pocket. I would catch you in an instant and butcher you into a million pieces." I believed him.

We walked in the sun, him right behind me. He controlled my body, but not my thoughts. When we approached the tanning salon he leaned in close again. "Just smile and look polite and happy, otherwise I will kill you as soon as we get out of here." I didn't feel like me anymore. I had so much fear pulsing through my body that I was frozen. I was just a marionette being controlled by Tomas. I would do whatever he said to make it easier on myself and to stay alive. I lay on the tanning bed, withering further to who I was before.

# First Trick

It was easy for me to lose track of time as Tomas's slave. My moments were not my own. For Tomas and his friends, life was a continual party. There was always loud music playing, and plenty of drugs and alcohol. There were no neighbours to complain. For me, life was a living hell. Each day I was abused and sold. I didn't usually know what day it was. I had no phone, no watch, no access to the outside world. It came to a point where they no longer had to make me use drugs and alcohol. I used them willingly. It was better to numb myself to the horrible things that were happening to me every night.

There were quiet moments during each day, when I would resolve to survive and think about getting away, but the sun would fall and each night would bring new horrors. Tomas told me about girls like me; if they went to the police they were arrested. It's against the law to sell yourself for money. The police didn't care about whores like me. Tomas had several locks on the door. I had seen his collection of guns and knives. I was never alone. There would never be a chance for me to escape.

One day, one of Tomas's mates came to take me with him. I felt hopeful, but he held me tightly on the way to the car. "Where are we going?" I asked timidly. *What if he actually isn't Tomas's friend? What if he is going to save me?*

"We're going to mine. I can't bear to lie with you on that filthy mattress at Tomas's," he said. The contempt on his face was clear, which confused me. If I was so disgusting, why was he paying Tomas to rape me? I had barely slept since arriving in London. My body and mind were heavy; I couldn't even think of running anymore. I wouldn't have the strength to get far.

We entered his home and he passed me a glass of whisky. "Drink this so that you can relax," he said laughing. I looked around, seeing toys on the floor and a crib in the living room. He rushed me down the hall and into the shower. "Wash yourself. I'm not going to touch you while you're dirty," he commanded. Like Tomas, he kept watch at the door. When I was done, he steered me back down the hall to the couch next to the crib. "I don't want you where I lie with my wife," he said, as if that would make sense to me.

As I sat, he was quickly on me, groping me. I sat numb. "Come on now, don't just sit there like some dumb virgin who doesn't know what to do. You should be good at this by now."

"I don't feel well," I said. He ignored me, climbing on top of me and using his weight to force himself inside of me. I don't know how long it went on. I tried to escape by going somewhere else inside my head. Eventually he rolled off me, panting.

"Go on back to the shower," he said, "unless you want to save my scent until later." Robotically I walked back down the hall. I scrubbed myself again, though I knew I would never feel clean. He left me alone in the bathroom, and as soon as the curtain was closed, I burst into tears, sobbing and crying out to God in my head again. *Please, God, save me! I can't take this anymore! Please, God, save me from these animals!* I wanted to scream aloud, but I knew that I would be punished if I did so.

He took me in the car back to Tomas and as we parked, he looked at me with a smug smile on his face. He passed me a twenty-pound note. "Here, give this to Tomas, and make sure to tell him that I said you were a good girl." I was shocked – twenty pounds? It only cost twenty pounds to rape me?! I had seen dolls in the shops that cost more than that. I exited the car in shock; that smug face locked in my brain. Tomas was there to walk me up the steps as his mate pulled away from the kerb.

He turned to me as soon as we walked through the door. "Do you have something for me?" he asked.

I handed him the twenty-pound note. I saw a storm cross his face. "What is this? Are you laughing at me?"

"N-n-no," I stammered. I was so confused.

He pushed me against a wall, wrapping his hands around my neck. "Are you stealing from me? What's going on?" I gasped for breath and tried to express that twenty pounds was what I had been given.

"You stupid whore," he said, beginning to laugh. "Let this be a lesson to you. You better ask me how much money you should be getting. Sit down, this was just a lesson." He laughed and passed me a cigarette. To him the twenty pounds was a training session; a lesson for me to learn.

I stared, trying to understand what kind of a person Tomas was. He was beyond my comprehension. When I was alone I closed my eyes. *How will this life end?*

# Something in the Air

Although Tomas never talked to me when he wasn't insulting me or hurting me, I began to pick up on something over the next few days. Tomas was constantly taking calls, pacing the house and chain smoking. I tried to listen in as closely as I could, but the voices on the other end of the phone were muffled, and Tomas said as little as possible.

One day there was a knock on the door that caused Tomas to jump up. "Don't move," he said. I stayed seated near the TV, but my ears followed Tomas to the door. There was shouting.

I didn't recognise the voice at the door, but I could hear that a man was here to collect a debt from Tomas.

"Well if you can't pay up then I'll just take your new girl from you," the man shouted. "I'll make her work off your debt."

"No, I can pay. Just give me a couple more days," Tomas pleaded. Though I was terrified, it was satisfying to hear Tomas being talked down to, to be the one who was powerless. Fear numbed my body again; fear about where I would be taken, and how much worse it might be with another man. The voices dropped, the door slammed shut and I held my breath.

Tomas re-entered the room. He saw me waiting and began to scream. "You shouldn't be listening to other people's conversations!"

"I'm sorry," I said automatically.

"You better get ready to leave," he said. "Tomorrow I'm taking you to my house. But you better behave. I have no problem pushing you into traffic if you try anything stupid." He paced around in a panic. "Come sleep next to me. I can't risk you trying anything stupid," he said. He lay next to me, his hand across my stomach possessively. It wasn't long before he was snoring, but as he slept and I lay awake in fear, his grip never lightened.

———————— ✦ ————————

Morning came quickly. Tomas was quick to wake up and pack a bag. I could see his passport sticking out of his pocket, but I didn't know why he would need it. "Today you pretend that we are a happy couple. Don't even dream of acting weird," he threatened. He laughed to himself, "We are so in love." We headed into the street and began to walk past barbershops and garages through the Seven Sisters area of London. After about thirty minutes we reached an Underground train station. I was amazed, having never seen that before. "Off we go," he said, nudging me down the steps. He handed me an Oyster card. "Swipe this and go through the gate." He mimicked how to use the card to travel by the train.

The station was crowded with commuters. Though I was instructed by Tomas to look happy, surely someone would recognise the agony in my eyes, I thought. The train rushed into the station, bringing a warm draft and a musty smell. I eyed his pockets, knowing that there was at least one weapon there. Would I be fast enough to run? I knew the answer was no.

We were on the train for what felt like hours, Tomas keeping me close. Though it was crowded, no one saw me for who I was. I felt like I was marked by a scarlet letter, but to everyone else I was just a girl. Everyone was attached to a mobile device or reading material. We disembarked in a city and walked past high-rise buildings and a school. There was a large supermarket and I grew hungry. Tomas walked until he came to a row of houses. He turned to me. "We're here. My landlord may be home with his family, so stay silent." I nodded. Tomas was in control. We walked straight to a little room down the hall where he locked the door behind us.

"If you go to the bathroom, I go to the bathroom. You will not be alone. Understood?" I nodded again. What could I say? Of course I understood. He turned on a TV to an old western movie, chuckling at the screen. I looked at the tiny window, willing myself beyond it. We were close enough to a school that I could hear the children, their bursts of laughter and the sound of play. I knew that I would never again be a child.

I felt that I never really had been. If I closed my eyes I could remember moments of my life where I had been joyful: games on a playground, laughter with Carmen, encouragement from my writing teacher. The window seemed to grow smaller as I felt Tomas's hand on my neck. "We will wait here for my mates to call on us. Be smart. The better you behave, the better I will treat you."

Eventually he needed to use the bathroom. He left the room and I glanced around, noticing a safe in the corner and an envelope beside it. I jumped up to read the name. It was not addressed to Tomas, but to someone named Villius. When I heard a door close down the hall I jumped back onto the bed before Tomas came back.

We were in that little room for a couple of days. Tomas always slept with a heavy hand on my stomach. I slept in fits. I was never rested. I was always afraid. I was always fatigued. On the second or third day, he said we were leaving, so I put on my coat, grabbed my small bag and we waited on the kerb until a green car pulled up. "Get in," he ordered.

Inside the car were two men. Smoke filled the air. The men laughed, reaching out to fist-bump Tomas. "This is Darius," said Tomas, nudging his head towards a chubby older man with red cheeks. Darius held a lit cigarette in one hand and a bottle of vodka in the other. "That's Lukas," he said, pointing to the driver, who looked like a scrawny student. Darius and Lukas both looked at me like hungry wolves.

"You've got a fresh one this time, mate," said Darius with laughter. "Good for you!"

Darius looked at me again. "Buckle up. We've got a long drive to Leeds. You'll find out how you should really work. There will be plenty of customers itching to get their hands on a pretty thing like you."

My heart sank further. Though I knew that I was not being rescued, it hurt to hear about the horrors that were waiting. Despite all of the rapes I had survived, it wasn't getting any easier.

I scooted as far as I could towards the door. Lukas noticed, turning on the child lock. Russian music blasted through the speakers as we drove away from London, while the three men carried on as if they were at a school reunion, and were not in the act of slowly killing someone.

Rain hit the window as London faded behind us. I tried to read the signs outside, but they were rushing past and as the sky darkened I couldn't make out the words.

We drove into an industrial area and Darius turned to me. "Get ready, we're coming up to your new home." He laughed. Hate coursed through my blood. I wished with everything I had that he would take a slug of vodka and choke and die. Lukas pulled the car to the kerb in front of a run-down house next to a scrapyard. The remnants of an old sign were attached to the roof.

"Get your bag and get into the house before anyone sees us," said Tomas. The outside of the house was dim, but inside there were bright neon lights and a large sign that flashed "Massage – Sexy." There were mirrors everywhere. It was obvious that it was a brothel.

A woman's voice boomed, "Hello, boys! You back then? Who do you have with you?"

She walked down the stairs and saw me. "I'm Rita, who are you?"

"Esther," I mumbled.

"Well welcome," she said. I was so confused. How could she be walking around so cheerfully in a house of horror? The men walked down the hall as Rita took my hand. "Let me show you to your room," she said. She turned and saw the bewildered look on my face. "First time in this job?" she asked.

My eyes immediately filled with tears. "Oh no," she said, reaching out and wiping my cheeks, "You're one of them." She paused and looked behind to see that the men were gone. "You can't cry here, Esther. It won't help. I feel for you, I do, but there's nothing I can do to help you. I don't want to get involved. But take my advice ... just do what they say. Don't go kicking and screaming and making it worse for yourself. You aren't the first girl and you won't be the last, but I know you want to stay alive." The trickle of tears turned into a flood as she spoke to me so matter-of-factly. I was choking. "You need to go wash your face," she said, pushing me to a sink. I saw five locks on the door and a security camera.

After I stopped crying, Rita took me into a large room where Tomas and the others were. There was a large TV being used to monitor every room in the house, as well as every entrance into and out of the house. Tomas saw me and shouted. "Don't just stand there. I'm hungry. Get into the kitchen. I want soup and chicken." He pushed me roughly into the hall, while Rita sat down to have a drink with the men. I was confused. Was she working as a prostitute or was she one of them?

I found the kitchen and looked around. I was far from domestic but had experience from my foster family and the meals Tomas had made me cook, so I did the best that I could, remembering both Tomas's and Rita's words that compliance would be best for my survival. I continued to cry as I prepared their meal. *I am a slave now. This is my life now.* Though I had been living it, I still couldn't believe it. I could hear music blasting and their laughter from the back room as I wondered how long I would survive here.

I brought the food back to the room with the TV, where I was told to wait in the corner. "If there's any left, you can eat," Tomas said. I helped myself to some leftover potatoes when I was made to clear their plates. When I returned from cleaning up the kitchen the party was in full swing. Rita sat on Darius's lap laughing and curling into his red neck. She giggled as he whispered into her ear. I still didn't know how she fit into the equation.

Tomas called me over and handed me a glass. "Drink." I sipped the vodka slowly. "Get on with it," he said.

I took larger gulps. He handed me a cigarette. "I'm in a good mood, so smoke, but I won't be this nice to you forever." I sat back, quietly smoking the cigarette. I saw lines of white powder on the table. Tomas noticed me eyeing the drugs and took a bill out, rolling it up. He passed it to me. "Get on with it," he said, nodding to the lines. I bent down to snort one. When I sat back up I was light-headed and the room faded away. The ketamine was racing through my system, and for the first time since I had been in the UK, my fear faded into the background.

I sat in the background, watching the room in slow motion until Tomas had had enough.

"Let's go, can't leave you alone," he said. We walked up the stairs and into the room that Rita had shown me, where Tomas fell asleep with his arm hanging heavily over me as usual. I lay there for a long time knowing that it wouldn't be long before someone was using me again. I knew that there were locks on the door, and cameras and security. There was no way to get away. Again.

# A New Hell

———— ✦ ————

I woke to Tomas's rough nudges and daylight trickling in through the puny window. "Get up. You won't be sleeping all day like a princess. It's time for you to shower. Make sure you shave everything," he commanded. He walked me to the bathroom to monitor.

From the bathroom he walked me to the kitchen to make his breakfast. I saw him and the others putting together an ad for the paper, advertising a massage from a new girl. "From now on, you're called Ann," said Tomas. When the phone would ring, Darius or Rita would answer in a joyful tone and promise the best massage. I couldn't believe that the newspaper would advertise the sale of sex, but massages were legal and they knew what they were doing.

"Come here," said Rita when I was done cooking. "You need to know what to say and what address to give." I noticed that she changed her voice to a seductive tone whenever someone was calling.

During the day I was told to do laundry and clean the house, but when the sun began to fade in the sky, I was made to clean myself up again. I needed to be presentable. Then, with a knock on the door, my life got even worse.

Two scruffy men entered the house. One of them walked straight to me and pointed, "I want that one." *That one,* as if I were a flavour of ice cream or a pair of shoes. Tomas came out to negotiate prices.

"Fifteen minutes will be thirty pounds, half an hour will be sixty and the full hour is a hundred and twenty." The men looked at each other and looked me up and down, whispering to each other. The one who had pointed to me took out his wallet and passed a handful of money to Tomas. Tomas escorted us up the stairs and locked me in with the man.

It was dark in the room and dark in my heart. The man turned to me and demanded that I service him.

———————◆———————

To this day, removed and safe, I cannot bring myself to speak about the things that I was made to do in that brothel room. I feel disgusted, revolted and such shame. I remember their hands on me; their mouths on me. I remember every demand that was made of me. There is no amount of washing that I can do to clean my body of their imprint; the greedy ways their hands took hold of me.

The days passed in the same way. I would cook Tomas's meals, I would do his laundry and I would clean the house. Occasionally Tomas would take me into the city to use the tanning bed or to buy me new cheap lingerie for exciting the clients. At night I would be made to wash up and put on make-up. Then I would be raped, sometimes up to twenty men in an evening. I was constantly in pain, both physically and mentally. I was alive, but barely living. I cried out to God for rescue, but no help came, just a line of men who must have been dead inside. When my period finally came I felt relief. Surely I would get a bit of a break? I told Tomas and he laughed, handing me a sponge. "Shove this up there and carry on," he said. "There's no way I'm losing money because of a little blood."

Every day there was a new way to lose my dignity. Once Tomas woke me at three in the morning for a customer who had requested me. The man had used so many drugs that his eyes were completely black. I was afraid as he raped me. Afraid at how long this could last, and of how angry he might become if I upset him for any reason. When he finished he rolled off me and chucked a bag of coins at me. He laughed as I counted what was there to give to Tomas.

When I looked in the mirror I no longer saw myself. I rarely slept. I was made to drink and take drugs daily. The dark circles under my eyes grew larger and larger. Still I was made to smother my face in make-up and endure hell every night.

# Why?

---------◆---------

"Why didn't you run?" A defence lawyer once asked me accusingly. "Why? If it was so bad, and you didn't want to be there, why didn't you run?"

I looked back into the face of a woman, a stranger, who could never understand what I had endured. Tears ran down my face, choking me.

How do you explain what it is like to be owned? To live in constant fear. To be drugged, drowned in alcohol. To be so exhausted and afraid that you couldn't move. To be surrounded by darkness, evil and malice. To know that your captors had the means to murder you and wouldn't hesitate to do so. To be lost. To be dead inside.

"I couldn't," I cried. "I couldn't get away."

I wasn't the only one you know. Rita was forced to work too, but she seemed to have something going on with Darius, so sometimes she was with him, and sometimes she was working. She seemed to be on their good side, and never expressed the misery that I was feeling. She also had a bit of freedom. Though she slept at the house often, she was allowed to leave to meet clients in hotels and also had her own flat in the city.

I tried to plead with her once, but I was quickly shut down. "I wish I could help you, Esther, but I can't. And I'm not going to risk my life. Your life here is better than what it could be. Remember the Turkish pimps?"

I was often told of the Turkish pimps, who were rumoured to keep their women in dungeons. The Turkish pimps would keep me injected with heroin and I would be starved, surviving only on water and a little bit of mush, and I would be used and used until I shrivelled up and died in that cellar. The thought of the Turkish pimps immobilised me.

Tomas was a monster. He hated me. He made me a slave to do his chores, he sold my body every night and he treated me like I was less than human, but he was somehow less evil than the Turkish pimps.

---- ✦ ----

Despite its horror, I wanted my life. My hopes had not died completely. I cried in the shower every day, crying out to a God at whom I was growing angry. I beat my fists against the walls; the pain in my knuckles was an escape from the pain in my heart and the rest of my body. I thought about dying every day, grabbing a knife in the kitchen and slashing my wrists, but in the end I wanted my life.

Rita told me that she had seen Tomas flip before and give out a beating that can't be described, but as long as I kept on his good side I would survive, so I did what I could to stay on his good side.

Why didn't I run?

Because I could not get away.

# A Teacher

When I was with men I was monitored very closely. There were video cameras everywhere, and someone was always near the door. When a man left my room, Tomas would rush in instantly to search every corner. He was worried that I was hiding tips – that I would save up money to escape from him.

One night a young man came in who seemed a bit nervous. He tried making small talk with me.

"Why do you do this?" he asked.

I'm not sure why I spoke the truth. "I don't want to be here," I admitted. He let out a deep breath and continued to ask me questions. I was filled with fear. What if someone outside of the door had heard me?

"What would you like to be?" he asked.

"A teacher," I said. It was the first thing that came to my mind.

He stood up instantly. "I can't do this," he said. "I'm a teacher. I don't know why I'm here, but I know that I can't do this." He left quickly without saying another word to me.

Tomas rushed in. "What is the problem?"

"I guess he wasn't feeling well," I said.

"Loser. We kept his money," Tomas laughed.

That night I thought about the teacher. Someone out there knew that I was here, and that I didn't want to be.

A couple of nights later there was a loud knock on the door. "Answer the door!" Tomas yelled. I walked down the hallway and opened the door to a massive man. He came in quickly, looking around. He was chatting nervously when he pulled out a walkie-talkie and ordered whoever was on the other side to come in now. The room quickly filled with police officers. I was stunned and frozen.

Tomas rushed into the room and yelled at me in Eastern European, "Don't you dare say a word! If you tell them that you are here against your will I will kill you before they can stop me."

It was happening so fast and I began to cry. He yelled again in Eastern European, "I will kill you! I will kill you before they can save you!"

"Speak in English or we will arrest you!" the officer yelled. The officers walked us into the front room and sat us on couches. Tomas was there with two of the other blokes, but Rita had successfully hidden herself away.

A woman approached me. She looked me in the eye and said, "Tell me your name. Are you working here of your own free will or is someone here forcing you to do this?"

I could feel six eyes burning holes into me. I wanted to scream for help. Yes! Who would ever choose this for themselves? Please help me! But when I opened my mouth I looked at Tomas and knew that he would kill me. I spoke, "Yes, I am choosing to be here."

The woman's face changed as she stood up and looked at her colleagues. She looked so disappointed; surely if she looked into my eyes she could see that I needed her, but she said, "Let's go, boys. Another one who is looking for easy money." They looked at me with disgust, and Tomas with hate, as they slowly left the way that they came.

When the door shut Tomas and his mates cheered and began slapping each other on the back. "Well that was easy, wasn't it?"

"Got a good little whore here who knew just what to say." I sat, dead on the couch while they made plans.

Tomas turned to me. "You'll be going somewhere new tomorrow and you better hope they treat you as well as we do, I'd hate to see you dead." My heart was breaking, another new hellhole. *How could the police have just been here, and now they're not? How could they have left me behind?*

The boys and Rita began to party. The alcohol was flowing, there were lines of cocaine everywhere and they laughed and danced to raunchy music. Tomas gave me a drink and cocaine, which I gladly took to numb myself. "Get ready to show me a good time tonight," Tomas said. "I want to see what all the fuss is about."

My heart sank. I knew exactly what he meant. I went out to a screened-in porch with Rita, trying to glimpse the moon in the sky. I smoked and sat with my thoughts. *Tonight Tomas is going to rape me and then he is going to kill me. Is he going to make it quick or make it last? Is it possible that I could kill him first? Am I a killer? How can I get a knife without getting noticed?*

Rita saw me deep in thought. "Don't get any crazy ideas, Esther. You can't outsmart them. You really can't. Just do what you're told."

I looked at the barbed wire at the top of the fence. I was trapped. From the radio inside I could hear the beginning of the Journey song, "Don't Stop Believing". I had always thought that the song was trite, but the title hit me. I wanted to believe that I could keep on living. In that moment, I wanted to live.

When Tomas got tired of vodka and cocaine he grabbed me and walked me to another room. He looked at me with hatred and lust. "Men have been coming back for seconds and thirds. I want to know what all the fuss is about. Take off your clothes."

Though I had been raped too many times to count or remember, being raped by Tomas scared me even more deeply. I began to cry.

"Stop the tears, or I won't be able to stay excited."
I stood hesitating in the middle of the room, my eyes
darting to the door and window. "Let's get on with
it," he said. With a sudden burst of energy I sprinted
to the door. I'm not sure where I thought I was going,
but Tomas was quicker, grabbing me forcefully. He
slammed me into the wall and then used my hair to
drag me to the bed. He shoved me down and as I
cried on the mattress he took what he wanted from
me. When he slowed and finished I closed my eyes,
waiting for a burst of pain, expecting him to stab
me with the knife in his jeans, but he collapsed on
top of me, his arm always holding me in place on my
abdomen. "Sleep. Tomorrow is a big day for you."

He snored as I stayed awake, watching the dim light
out the window as it transitioned from moonlight to
sunlight, unsure if I really wanted to live or die.

# Back to London

In the morning a car was waiting for us. Tomas rushed his friends and me to gather our belongings and get into the car. We drove back to London. I had no explanation of what was going on. He seemed stressed, which didn't help my anxieties. I remembered all of the stories that I had been told about the Turkish pimps and sat quaking with fear. We pulled into the car park of a hotel, in a spot next to a black Range Rover with tinted windows. "Wait here," he said to me as he got out of the car and approached the window of the Range Rover. He talked briefly and then opened the door for me. "Get into that car," he said. "Now." I had learned by now never to question him, so I quickly slid out with my backpack and into the back seat of the Range Rover. When I glanced out the window, Tomas was already driving away.

My eyes adjusted to the darkness within the car. There were several well-dressed men.

The tall one in the front turned to me and said, "We expected you over a month ago. Where have you been?"

"Leeds," I answered.

"What the hell were you doing in Leeds?"

"He took me there and made me work for him," I said.

"That scum. He was supposed to bring you straight to us. No wonder he was in such a rush to pass you off to us," he answered. There was amusement in his voice. Though these men looked better off than Tomas, I knew that I was in the same situation. They had purchased me. Tomas had just chosen to make money off me first.

That night we went to a bar. The drinks were flowing and the cocaine was abundant. At this point I accepted it readily. It helped me to cope. Perhaps I had grown addicted. Either way, I didn't hesitate when it was offered to me. "We'll show you how to party, Esther," one of the men said.

Within minutes the bar was locked down, emptied out except for the men I was with and the owner of the pub. Though the night passed in a blur I saw how the owner of the pub cowed to these men. I could tell that they were far more powerful and respected than Tomas.

Towards the morning they were running out of cigarettes. Their eyes met and a silent conversation was held. My passport was held out to me. "You look young. You'll need this to go pick up more ciggies." I took it timidly, wondering why they would offer me moments of freedom.

I walked outside to the shop, which was right by the pub. My mind was racing. *Surely this is a test. The shop is too close to the pub for me to get away. If I try and fail I will be killed. If I try, I will fail. I know that.*

I got the cigarettes as requested and returned to the pub. "Here you go," I said.

The leader, Xander, retrieved them. "As long as you listen you will be treated well here. If you try to play us, we will end you." I nodded in understanding. They didn't ask for my passport back, which felt like another test. In one night I could see that they were well connected and powerful men. *Where can I run so that I can escape them?*

When they got tired of partying, we went to a hotel. I was given a chance to shower, change clothes and rest. Unlike Tomas, they told me what was going to happen to me.

"Tomorrow night you'll be going to a brothel. Johnny's mum owns it and you'll be working there," said Xander.

I slept. Xander didn't try to rape me, though he did stay close. I didn't feel safe, but I was at least kept aware of what was going on.

The next night he cut two large lines of cocaine and told me to take one.

In the car we drove through the city, bright with lights. It was beautiful. Through the window I saw expensive cars, well-dressed people on the pavements and a posh hotel. This street was totally different from where I had been spending my time. When we arrived and parked, I was escorted up a wide staircase to an apartment in the sky. For a moment I felt surprised that a brothel was operating in this part of town, but then realised that these men were probably looking for more power – and to buy sex.

The door opened quickly and a woman was waiting there for us. I could tell immediately that she was trying desperately to cling to her youth. Her bleached blonde hair and skimpy dress belonged on a teenager and weren't fooling anyone. "I'm Inga," she said. "Follow me."

We walked down the hallway to a room. "This is where you'll be sleeping." She handed me a dress similar to her own. "Put this on and make yourself presentable. The clients will be arriving soon." I waited for her to leave me alone, but she stood still. "Go ahead, I'm waiting," she said.

I changed quickly and smoothed my hair, not bothering to look in the mirror. I didn't want to see myself. "Let's go," she said. I followed her back down the hall and into a sitting room. When we entered, the room froze. A few girls were chatting with one another, but they stopped when they saw Inga. "This is Esther. She'll be working here and that's all you need to know. Don't go asking her any questions. If you have any queries, you come to me. Understand?" They nodded. Nobody welcomed me. I sat on the corner of a couch. When Inga left the room, the chatting resumed. The other girls avoided me, as if Inga's warning had scared them. Xander and Johnny were still there, and the alcohol and cocaine were abundant. I listened carefully. From what I understood, the others were there by choice, working as escorts and giving a portion of their proceeds to Inga.

The entry-phone rang and Inga came into the room. "Hush now and have a seat," she said.

"Smile, the customers are coming." She left to answer the door, and I could hear her greeting people.

"Welcome, come on in." She entered the room with a man in a suit and shiny shoes. From the neck down he looked like a nice man, but his face showed that he had been drinking, and he was ready for more. The other girls crossed the room to him, rubbing his arm and laughing. I could not find the strength to stand and couldn't understand why they were rushing to be with this man.

"Take your pick," Inga said with a smile. He looked around like a kid in a candy store. He grabbed a blonde by the hand and led her down the hall. Inga came straight to me and said, "Listen, I don't know your story, and I don't care. This is a brothel. You are here to make money. You have to smile and chat up the customers so they want to be with you. You must earn a certain amount of money for us each week or things will get worse. I will let my son do whatever he wants to you. You don't want that. Understand?"

"Yes," I said timidly.

"I used to be like you, scared and whatever. But look at me now. I run the place. If you play it right you can be like me." With that she turned and walked away. I sat back down. My mind was blown. *How could a woman*

*do this to other women? How could a woman be so*
*dark? I guess money really does change people.*

It wasn't long before I was chosen; when I was taken
by the hand and led down the hall. Occasionally,
one of the men would want nothing more than to do
cocaine and talk to me, as if I was some sort of sexy
therapist, but I didn't mind. I could survive to myself if
I wasn't being forced to trade sex for money. Being at
Inga's was no different from being with Tomas and his
friends. The suits were nicer and so was the apartment
but having sex for survival isn't a life. I died more and
more each day, with each customer seeing me as less
than human.

The girls there were a bit like Rita, coming and going
of their own free will. I was the only one being kept
captive. I was the youngest and my English was poor,
so other than the occasional drink or cigarette, the
others kept away from me. Inga had warned them
against getting close to me, and people did what
she said.

I looked out of the windows during the day, at the
lovely streets of London. I hoped. I dreamed. And I did
what I had to do to survive.

# Andy

Andy was a taxi driver from Ghana. He would bring well-dressed men to Inga's to purchase us for an hour or so. Andy was always very chatty, but I was withdrawn and had a hard time carrying on a conversation.

Everything changed between us one night when Inga left for an hour. She put one of the other girls, Natasha, in charge, and Andy moved closer to me on the couch.

"I'm not stupid, you know. I can tell that you don't want to be doing this," he said quietly.

"I don't want to be here, but it isn't really my say," I answered honestly.

"Look, I know how these places work," he said.

"What do you mean?"

He cleared his throat. "I heard Inga talking a few days ago. You aren't making enough money. If things don't change, they are going to get rid of you."

"No," I said in fear.

He cut a line of coke for me. "Take this. You can barely hold your head up." I leaned down and took the drugs, waiting for the immediate rush to follow. I lifted my head and met his eyes. He continued. "They will get rid of you, Esther, but it won't be alive. If they get rid of you they are going to kill you and cut out your organs. They can fetch up to ten thousand dollars for you that way. Did you know that?"

I nodded. I did know that. I remembered a conversation that Inga had been having on the phone a few days prior. In whispered tones she had discussed the price of human organs as if they were pieces of produce. "What do I do?" I asked, shaking in fear.

He lowered his voice again. "We can do something about it, but we have to act here and now. Inga is not here, but she almost always is. Go grab your things and leave with me. Natasha can 'fall asleep' and we can get away."

I stood and walked to my room, my mind racing. I knew I wasn't earning enough here, because it was physically impossible for me to look happy about sleeping with these men. On the one hand, I barely knew Andy; on the other, I knew that I would die if I stayed. I didn't have much with me. I had my backpack and, miraculously, my passport. I grabbed both and returned to Andy.

"We need to go now. She could be back any minute," he said.

I looked at Natasha. "Go," she said, looking away.

Andy grabbed me by the arm and we rushed down the back staircase to his taxi. In the car he reached out and patted me on the leg. "Don't worry," he said. "Natasha won't tell, and where I'm taking you they will never find you."

"Where are we going?" I asked.

"To my brother's house," he said. We sat in the quiet and drove for about an hour. I saw a sign welcoming us to Catford. I didn't know where we were or what was going to happen to me next.

# A Change of Pace

Andy drove to a neighbourhood full of terraced houses packed tightly together. He continued to chat. "You aren't the first one I've helped, you know. I once helped another girl – I think she's from the same country as you – and she ended up getting on so well with my other brother that they are getting married soon! You'll meet her. They live in Daniel's house too." He parked on the kerb in front of a yellow house, smiling.

There were several voices as we entered the house and I was introduced to Daniel, Tony and a thin young woman named Anna. They smiled freely. We walked to the couch and Anna spoke. "Andy called to tell us you were coming, but I didn't think it would be so quick. You smoke?"

"Yes," I answered.

She reached out, passing a cigarette to me. "Here you go. Have a seat." I sat and backed myself into a corner. "So what brings you here?"

I had worked out that she was the girl whom Andy had rescued. "Same as you, I guess."

"Ah, I see. I guess you don't want to talk about it."

"No, I don't," I said. We sat back in a comfortable silence. The brothers chatted in another room.

When Andy came back into the room he looked at me. "Look, I gotta go. I need to go home and get back to driving to Inga's so that it doesn't look suspicious. They will take care of you. Don't worry."

"OK," I said. When he left I felt afraid, but it was good.

"You want a bath?" Anna asked.

"Yes," I said. She walked me down the hall and gave me a towel. Then she shut the door and walked away. *She shut the door.* This may not seem like a big deal, but I had not showered alone since I was in Eastern Europe. When I got out I was given a meal and during the remainder of the day I was left alone.

That night Tony and Anna went into the room after saying goodnight, and Daniel turned to me. "You can share my bed," he said. "There is nowhere else for you to sleep." My heart sank as I followed him into the room. *So this is where I will be raped,* I thought. But to my surprise he said goodnight to me and then turned away, his back to me. I lay as still as possible beside him, not quite trusting the situation. It took me ages to fall asleep, but it was quiet there and I eventually calmed myself down and fell asleep.

When I awoke the sun was shining brightly through the window. I found Anna in the kitchen and saw the clock on the stove. It was noon and I had been left alone! "You must be starving," Anna said. "Let me make you a plate." It had been a long time since I was treated with dignity, and I willed the tears back from the corners of my eyes. "Sleep good?" she asked.

I nodded with my mouth full of toast. "Yes," I mumbled.

"Andy left some money for you so that we can do a bit of shopping today. He knows you don't have much with you, and you'll need something to wear."

I couldn't believe it, but I nodded and said politely, "Thank you." It was hard to eat. I hadn't been sober in weeks and I was shaking. Things seemed too good to be true. As I ate and dressed, I fought off suspicions. Anna and the brothers had been nothing but kind to me, but something still felt off. Maybe I would never feel right again.

I dressed and we walked out into the sun. I looked around, fear creeping into my chest. "It's OK," said Anna. "London is a huge city. Your pimps won't find you here. They probably have already found another girl to take your place. You can relax."

I couldn't, but I tried to appear as if I had. I looked around me, willing myself to appreciate the sun, the wind on my face, the birds chirping. I wasn't alone, but Anna wasn't like Inga or Rita. *I am free. This could truly be over.* I picked out loose and comfortable clothing with Anna.

When we returned to the house I was exhausted. Even though it was only four in the afternoon, I crawled into Daniel's bed and fell asleep. When I woke up it was morning and I was not alone in the bed. I panicked.

*Tomas is beside me.* I fought off a scream and opened my eyes to see Daniel's back. He had crawled into bed beside me, but he had turned away from me again and left me alone.

For the next couple of days we got into a routine. Tony and Daniel would leave to work, and Anna and I would stay home and watch TV. She would ask me questions about my plans, but I didn't know what to tell her. She told me about herself. "I have a kid back in Eastern Europe," she confessed.

"What happened?" I asked.

"My ex and I came here to London a few years ago. When we got here he turned nasty. When we needed money, he made me work at Inga's, and when he was angry he beat me. It got worse and worse, until I met Andy and he brought me here."

"But what about your son?"

"Well, I got on with Tony once I got here, and soon we are going to get married. I'm going to bring my son here after that."

I nodded in understanding. I watched her with Tony. It seemed like an act. They didn't argue or anything, but it didn't seem like they were in love. But who was I to judge?

"So what do you think you'll do? Where do you think you'll go?" she asked. I shrugged, I didn't know. I had no money and I knew nothing about London. "Well," she said. "You are lucky that Andy saved you. He may just seem like a taxi driver, but Andy is a powerful man. He saved your life, so make sure you show your gratitude to Andy and Daniel," she said.

"I will," I said.

That night when the men got home we had dinner at the table and it was decided that we would go out on the town for some drinks. "We have been working hard, we need to chill out a bit," Tony said.

"Yes," Daniel agreed, winking at me.

We went to the pub and the drinks began to flow. With the vodka back in my system I began to settle a bit. After shots Daniel put his arm around me and pulled me close. I tensed, and he felt it. "Relax. We are here for a good time," he said.

Anna smiled. "I think he likes you," she whispered to me, like two schoolgirls discussing a crush.

I laughed and didn't respond. *Don't they know where I'm coming from? I'm not interested in being liked by anyone.*

Later Anna sat by me in a booth. She took another shot and turned to me. "If I were you, Esther, I'd just entertain Daniel. Don't forget that Andy took you out of that brothel."

"Yeah, but . . ." I trailed off.

"You need to show your gratitude somehow. And besides, think about it. Isn't it better for you to just be with one man, and not have to go back to the brothel and be passed from man to man."

"Yes, but . . ." I couldn't respond.

"That's what I do with Tony. He's only one man and he doesn't beat me. I have my freedom to leave the house." She looked at me as if my future had already been determined.

"So you don't love him?" I asked.

"Love!?" she laughed. "You are living in La-La Land. Listen, Esther. Tony and Daniel are here on a visa from Ghana, but it's expiring soon. To stay they need to get married. So we are safe now and we can help them out too. It's better than a brothel. And once we are married I will see my son again." She smiled at the thought. *But what about me? I don't have a child that I need to be reunited with . . .*

"Yes," I agreed, but I was shaking my head. *Lies. Lies. Lies. I knew it had been too good to be true. Of course, no one would want to help me simply for the sake of doing the right thing.*

I continued on partying, but my mind and heart were in a battle. If I didn't stay with Daniel, what would become of me? I could not go back to Eastern Europe. I had no money. Anna's words were in my head. Yes, one man was better than twenty, but for me, one was too many. I didn't ever want to be touched by a man. They disgusted me.

Still, being with Daniel seemed like my only choice. I would have to live a lie to have a roof over my head. My fate seemed decided. When we got home we continued to drink and Daniel kissed me. I turned to Anna. "Go with it," she said. "This is the best way, Esther."

That night in bed Daniel did not turn his back to me. He ran his hand over my stomach and I shuddered. I waited for him to put his weight on top of me. When the time came he grunted like all of the others and I squeezed my eyes shut to keep from crying.

From then on Daniel considered me his girlfriend and I considered myself a fake. I cooked his meals and did his laundry. Anna and I kept the house clean, and time passed as I tried to figure out what to do to truly be free.

# Natasha

As Anna and Tony's wedding approached, I learned more about her. She was marrying Tony for safety, and for five thousand pounds, but as the wedding grew closer she grew sadder. The men started to realise that it might not be easy to make the wedding look real if Anna's side was empty, so I was given a role to play. I would be Anna's old friend from school, and I would stand by her side as her witness. *More lies.* We visited the church and I saw that Anna was not a cheerful bride, but I went along with it. She knew that they would have to remain married for five years for Tony to get his visa. She wanted her safety and her son. I just wanted to stay out of the brothel, so I went along with it.

A few days before the wedding, Andy came to see us and gave us a pile of money. "Tomorrow my wife will pick you up and take you shopping and for haircuts." Andy seemed like a father to Tony and Daniel. Who knew if they were even related? I was used to everything being a lie. We accepted thankfully, knowing that we needed to look the part.

When his wife Natasha arrived the next day, I was blown away. She was a drop-dead gorgeous woman.

I recognised her as Russian, and someone who carried herself with pride and elegance – the kind of woman you don't want to mess with. When we had a moment, Anna nudged me and whispered, "Keep your distance. Natasha is not like us and she doesn't know where Andy is when he's working."

"OK," I said.

"She doesn't know about the cocaine or Inga's place, and he'd be furious if she found out all of that because of you. He'd take you back for sure." She narrowed her eyes at me, ensuring my silence.

I nodded. I wouldn't betray his secret. We enjoyed the day as best we could, though my mind spun at the quantity of lies I was carrying.

On the wedding day, we were picked up by a Hummer limousine that Andy had ordered. Even though the relationship was fake, you could tell that Andy wanted Tony to have a great day. I dressed in my new dress and stood by Anna's side with a smile on my face. Anna stood proudly next to Tony, faking it well. About ten of us exited the wedding and climbed back into the limousine. I noticed the vodka sitting there and quickly accepted when a drink was pressed into my hand. We turned up the music and drove around the city at the height of sophistication. We drove around the city for hours, drinking, singing and occasionally stopping for smoke breaks. I almost felt happy. Daniel kept trying to hug me, but I guess my discomfort was noticeable because Anna whispered in my ear, "Just play your part, Esther, and he'll play his."

The limousine pulled up at a relative's house and we bounced inside to continue the celebration. Andy spoke to me quietly, "Come with me." I followed him down the hall to the bathroom. Once inside he closed the door and pulled out a bag of coke. "You don't seem to be too happy, Esther. Maybe this will help," he said. I nodded and watched as he cut the lines. As soon as it hit my bloodstream I felt a release of tension. My hands, feet and head felt light, and I felt a rush through my body. I had no worries. I enjoyed the night, a young girl at a party without a care in the world.

———————— ✦ ————————

The next morning, reality returned. When I woke Daniel was sitting there angrily, and he stomped from the room. I rolled over and closed my eyes, I needed more sleep. I heard the door again and looked through half-closed eyes to see Anna at the foot of the bed. She opened a can of beer and held it out to me. "Here. This will help you with the hangover," she said.

"Thanks," I groaned.

"Listen," she said. "We need to talk." I nodded and waited. "It hasn't gone unnoticed around here the way that you've been treating Daniel. Tony let it slip yesterday that Andy is mad and he's thinking about taking you back to where you came from."

Fear smacked me to complete sobriety. "How long can I keep this up, Anna? How long will I have to play this game? How long? I can't pretend to like him or be someone's girlfriend anymore. I don't want him touching me. I feel sick each time he looks at me, and each time he gets in bed I have to pretend to be asleep. I can't do this! I can't just keep giving my body away. It's disgusting!"

"Shhhh," she said, looking at me seriously. "You haven't got much choice here, Esther. Women like you and me have to stick to the rules to survive. I don't want to do this as much as you don't, but outside this house there's nothing for you. Here at least you have protection. Where will you go? You know no one; you barely know the language; you don't even know the city! If you go away, it will be no time before either the Eastern Europeans find you or you will get sent back to Eastern Europe where the mob will eventually catch up with you and you will get what they think you deserve." I shook my head, but I knew that she was right. "This is our life," she said.

I gathered my last bit of strength. "I can't do it," I said. I left the room and walked to the kitchen to light a cigarette on the stove. My mind raced, but it went in circles. It didn't seem as if there was a way out. So I continued to drink as much as possible, and do cocaine when it was available. When I was drunk or high it was easier for me to let Daniel touch me. The days continued to pass.

One day Natasha came by the house unexpectedly, a vision of beauty and grace. "I came to take you for a girls' night," she said gleefully. Anna and I followed her to the car; Anna giving me looks of warning to fake my part as always. Natasha took us to a fancy Thai restaurant. I was overwhelmed with the beauty and the food. I didn't eat much because the food didn't make sense to me, but I drank and drank until I nearly fell off my chair. I excused myself to the bathroom, feeling shame as I looked in the mirror. Here I was with Natasha, but I was a mess. I wore a stained hoodie, my hair was unwashed and there was dirt underneath my nails. I didn't fit in with this type of woman with her perfect hair and make-up. My internal voice began to bash me. *Look at you. You're worthless. You'll never fit in with women like these. You are nothing.*

The door to the bathroom swung open and Natasha entered, smiling. She saw me frozen in place and her face showed concern. "Are you OK, Esther?" she asked.

I stood still. She continued, "Look, I know something isn't right here. There is something wrong, but I can't figure it out. I need you to tell me!"

"I can't," I said. "I wish I could, but I can't."

"Look, Andy is my husband, but there is something that I can't figure out. I know that he is gone late at night, working, but when he comes home he is drunk and high. And that woman Anna is coming across as controlling. Don't think I haven't noticed that she won't let you be alone with me. Tell me while you have the chance!"

I opened my mouth, but the door swung open again and Anna was there. Her eyes took in the situation.

"Come on, girls, food is ready. What's taking you so long?" she asked.

"Just fixing our make-up," said Natasha.

"Well I'll just go to the bathroom while you finish up," said Anna. She closed the door to the stall. Natasha put her finger to her lips and passed me a piece of paper. I nodded my understanding and put the paper into my pocket.

"Come on, Anna. Now who's taking a long time?" Natasha teased.

"I'm coming!" Anna shouted.

For the remainder of dinner I felt the weight of the paper in my pocket. I couldn't eat. I just pushed rice around my plate and drank. From the restaurant we went to a club, where the glittering lights blinded me. I had never been to a place like that, with shining lights and beautiful people on the dance floor. Anna stayed close, not allowing Natasha and me to be alone again.

When Natasha saw someone she knew and went away, Anna leaned in.

"So what were you two talking about?" she asked.

"Nothing," I lied. "She was just asking if I was hung over after the wedding."

"Good," said Anna. "Don't forget what I told you. Don't get close to her. She isn't one of us. You need to be careful."

"I know," I said, ending the conversation.

It took ages before Anna finally left us alone. "Do you know where Anna came from?" I asked Natasha.

"No," she said. "But by the way she acts and the speed at which she got married to Tony, I'm starting to think that it's all a lie."

I knew that there were only seconds before Anna returned, so I gathered my courage. "I know you know that Andy is a driver. What you don't know is that he is a driver for a brothel. He 'rescued' Anna and me so that his brothers could get married and have a visa." I expected a look of shock on her face, but she was calm.

"Right. Look, we need to do something about this now. I don't trust Anna, but I can see that you want help. We need to go." She grabbed my arm and began to pull me towards the exit. I could see Anna's back to us from across the club. In no time we were outside and hailing a taxi. When we shut the door, she turned to me again. "Look, I have a child with Andy, and I don't really want him to carry on with this mess. It's going to get him killed. But right now let's focus on you. I have cousins in Ireland who can help us. I will deal with Andy and Anna later. Right now we'll just go back to my place. I have to grab a few things."

I was in shock. I couldn't believe that Natasha wanted to help me. It took about twenty-five minutes in the taxi. She kept looking at her phone and mumbled, "We better pray that Anna hasn't told Andy yet and that he isn't on his way." I wanted to throw myself at her feet in gratitude, but I sat frozen in place.

We pulled up to the kerb and we walked quietly to the door. When she opened the door we couldn't hear anything. I exhaled, not even knowing that I had been holding my breath. She motioned for me to follow her and began to climb the stairs. It was quiet, then suddenly there was a loud bang and a huge shadow was rising up. The shadow moved into the light and I could see that it was Andy with his hands around Natasha's neck. She struggled as he began to yell, "What the hell are you doing going behind my back? Why would you risk our safety by bringing her here? Thankfully Anna rang me and I got here on time. I was only trying to help that ungrateful slut by taking her away from her pimps! I guess that was the biggest mistake of my life." Natasha was shaking her head but was silent.

Suddenly he released his grip, shoving Natasha to the side and rushing down the stairs to where I was frozen to the spot. "You only had to keep your mouth shut and get on with it! But it seems you even mess that up, you idiot!" I turned to run to the door and he screamed, "Where do you think you're going? You don't even know where you are! Come here now before I lose my patience and beat the hell out of you!"

I knew that he was right. I had no clue where to go, nothing in my hands and a story that I doubted people would believe. I stopped. He pointed to the car with authority and then turned back to Natasha, "I'll deal with you later. Go to sleep now." She nodded in defeat. Then he turned to me, "We are going for a little ride."

I trembled in the car as he made his way around. He looked furious, and I grew more and more afraid as he revved his engine and began to spew his anger at me. "Why did you have to be like that? All you had to do was be nice to my brother. You had a roof over your head and us backing you! Of course my brother won't want you anymore after this, and we can't trust you to keep the police away." The neighbourhood became clear outside of the window. We were nearing his brother's house. I could see Daniel coming down the path with a rubbish bag in his hand. He opened the door and threw the bag at me, his eyes full of hate. I could see some of my belongings through a hole in the side.

Andy pulled away again and began to drive. I wanted to explain myself, but I didn't know what to say. My experiences were heavy, and he lacked compassion. How could I explain that sleeping with Daniel was just as painful as being sold to strangers? I didn't want to be with any man. How was that so hard to believe? How could he not understand? My mind was still thick with vodka, but I could tell from the street signs that we were headed towards central London. I panicked as I realised that we were headed back to the brothel.

"Please don't make me go back! Please! Please just drop me off on the side of the road. I will just disappear."

"Do you think I'm stupid? Of course I'm not taking you there! If I did that, they'd realise that I was the one who helped you to get away! No, I have another use for you."

"Please, Andy," I begged.

He turned to me with hate in his eyes. "Shut up. Your tears do nothing to me. Don't you realise that your stupidity got you here? Your life is in my hands. So, just shut up and do as I say!"

He parked the car and grabbed my bag. "Follow me." I did as he said, following him up a path and into a private garden. He knocked and a large African woman opened the door. A man was behind her. He and Andy began to talk in their native tongue and my mind swirled. I had no idea what was being said. He then turned back to me. "You now belong to my uncle. You will do as you're told. Let's not forget that you're basically across the street from your pimps, so if you try running away, they are likely to find you. I'm sure that you don't want that." He turned and walked away.

The woman grabbed me by the elbow and led me into the kitchen. I sat at the table and she passed me something to drink. I saw girls in dresses that barely covered anything and knew that I was in another brothel. The woman spoke to me gently. "Well how did you find your way here? I can see that you are shaking. What is your story? I'll see what I can do."

I had nothing to lose, so I began to talk. I told her everything while she listened quietly.

When I was finished she said, "Right. Well tonight you can drink as much as you like. If anyone walks in here and sees you, just smile. Then you will rest. There is a room in the back. When my uncle arrives tomorrow he will give you directions as to what to do next."
I nodded in understanding. I felt relief that I would not be sold immediately.

I drank heavily, observing the house. Men and women came and went. Piles of cash were handed back and forth. No matter how much I drank, it felt as if I couldn't get drunk enough to have a sense of peace. My fear kept me in a panic. When it began to grow light outside and I could hear the cleaning trucks brushing the streets, the woman took me to a back bedroom and told me to sleep. *If you sleep and get rested, you will be able to make sense of this situation,* I told myself. I tossed and turned, but eventually found myself drifting into sleep.

The child in me thought that if I kept my eyes closed, nothing bad could happen to me.

# A New Normal

———— ✦ ————

I awoke to the sound of hair being brushed. My head was splitting in half, but I could see through my half-closed eyes that a girl was brushing her hair at the vanity. I turned my head from side to side and took in my surroundings. There were four single beds, a vanity and a dresser. We were alone. When the girl noticed me stirring, she spoke, "Hey there. You must be new. I'm Sophia. What's your name?" She was smiling, which felt so out of place.

"I'm Esther," I answered, my voice cracking. The party from the night before had left me feeling and sounding poorly.

"Hi, Esther. It's already evening time. You slept quite a while," she said, still sounding joyful. I was confused by her demeanour. How could she seem so happy in this situation? I was starting to feel fear for the night ahead when the door cracked open. It was the woman from the night before.

"Time to get up and at 'em, Esther. The clients will be coming soon. You'll need to get cleaned up in the bathroom and throw on some make-up. Tonight you will serve as hostess and then we'll see what's what when Uncle gets here."

I dragged myself to the bathroom to take a shower, my head splitting as I stood. I saw a beer on the table and helped myself to it. I would need it to have the energy to survive the shower.

There were plenty of women milling around as I scrubbed up and put on make-up. I was the only one who appeared to be sad about our circumstances. The others were drinking and talking, doing lines of cocaine. Women arrived from the outside, which made my head spin. *Why in the world would anyone be here voluntarily? How could women sell themselves of their own free will?* The woman returned to explain the expectations. "Tonight you will greet our guests and serve them drinks. Make sure that they are comfortable and that they have everything they want immediately." I nodded my consent, grateful that I would be given this role.

When the waiting began, I was able to distract myself temporarily. About fifteen women sat chatting. When a pair saw me eyeing the cocaine on the table, they laughed and passed me the crumpled-up bank note. I accepted it gratefully. The drug hit the back of my throat and the bitter taste was welcome to me. I accepted a cigarette. I felt dizzy and satisfied, like I was somewhere else, not in a trashy living room waiting to be sold without my permission.

The door opened and Uncle appeared. He was large and larger than life, greeting everyone boisterously in a strong Ghanaian accent. "Hello, my girls! Are we ready to make some money tonight?" He clapped his hands together as the girls responded in affirmation.

"You there! New girl!" he pointed to me. "You know where the fridge is? Go and get everyone some drinks. The party starts now!"

As I rose, he wedged himself between two women on the couch, wasting no time in running his large hands over their thighs. I felt bile in the back of my throat, and anger. I could hear Sophia and her friend laughing at his stupid jokes, seemingly numb to the groping of this pervert.

In the fridge I found beer, cider and champagne. I grabbed them all to bring to the table.

Uncle saw me, his face lighting up. "Bring me a beer, new girl!" I handed it to him and he laughed again. "Aren't you going to open it for me?" I wanted to smash the bottle over his head, but I did what he said. For the next hour I did my job, serving drinks and lighting cigarettes, until the phone rang. Uncle turned down the music to answer.

"My man! What can I do for you tonight? (Pause) You know I have everything that you need, ha ha. (Pause) Yes, the Portuguese is here, and I have a wide range of others, which you can see for yourself when you arrive! (Pause) OK, see you soon, my friend." He hung up and turned to us. "We have a new customer tonight. Make sure that you are smelling good, and smiling, like always. New girl, go make sure that the back bedroom is ready and that there are refreshments waiting on the side table." I nodded my head and went to do as he said. I saw that the room was prepared with crisp fresh bedding.

The doorbell rang as I returned to the room. Uncle looked at me. "Go on, new girl. Answer the door with a smile and welcome him as if he is royalty." I headed to the door. "Don't forget to offer him a drink and show him here." I opened the door to a taxi driver and a tall gentleman in a suit.

"Hello," I said. "Can I get you something to drink?" They followed me without response. When we got to the living room they asked for drinks. When I returned from the kitchen, the man was surrounded by women, clearly intoxicated and chatting freely.

Uncle returned to the room as well. "Come on now, man. Take your pick from these sluts that are happily here waiting for you." The man looked around, taking a brunette by the hand.

Uncle clapped his hands together joyfully, leading them down the hall himself. "Have a wonderful night," he said as he closed the door. He beckoned me to follow him to the kitchen, where he dumped a bag of cocaine onto a silver tray. "Make lines. You can have one, then take the rest to the back room. Make sure to knock first."

"Yes," I replied.

"And make sure to ask if he wants anything else," added Uncle. I nodded, following his instructions.

This was my new normal. When would I be free?

My new routine settled in around me over the next few weeks. In the morning I would wake up at about eight and clean the flat. It seemed as if I was preparing a holiday getaway for the men who frequented it at night, changing the sheets, tidying up and destroying any evidence of wrongdoing from the night before. Then I would prepare a meal for Uncle. After lunch I would shower and get myself ready, then make Uncle a second meal before the other ladies began to arrive. The woman who had greeted me on the first night was Uncle's much younger girlfriend, but he shared his affections when she wasn't around.

There were a whole slew of women coming and going, but Sophia was my favourite. She was the closest thing to a friend that I had had in a while. I gathered through our chats that she came from Brazil and used every penny she made to support her two sons back home. She was in the country illegally, on an expired visa, and she loved her family. She had their pictures in her phone and would share them with me when no one was around. Her face would light up with love in her eyes. I tried to share my story with her as well, but it came out in snippets. The other women couldn't be trusted. Everyone wanted to impress Uncle, to get in his favour and get richer clients, so I kept myself from them.

Sophia always had liquor and cocaine. I know that's how she coped with what she was doing, and I used them to numb myself as well. I almost started to feel guilty there as Uncle's slave. *Am I just as bad as him for knowing what is going on? Is it wrong of me to feel relieved that I'm not made to sell my body like the others?*

When the men came, I answered the door with a smile. I took their orders and prepared their drinks and their drugs. I kept the rooms in service.

It was naive of me to believe that it would continue that way.

One morning Uncle and I were alone in the flat. "I want to party," he said. I could see in his eyes what he was thinking. He had the same sleazy look that the men had each evening. My blood ran cold, but I brought tequila at his request. He was much bigger and stronger than me. My life was literally in his hands. We drank and drank. My thoughts were two-fold, *If I am drunk, I may survive this; but if he is drunk, he may fall asleep and forget about his plan to use me.*

"So how is your life going, Esther?" he asked. It seemed comical that he tried to make conversation with me, as if my life really mattered to him. I matched him shot for shot, but he remained alert. I remained sober, no matter how hard I tried to numb myself. Eventually he got to what I knew was coming, "Come with me to the room." My feet dragged behind me.

"I don't want to sleep with you," I said.

"Come now. You don't want to make things harder for yourself," he answered. The room at the back was painted a bright orange colour and the curtains were tightly shut. He pulled me to him and removed my pants. I gulped, fighting back the tears that were surely to come. I shook my head no, but he didn't care. He used his meaty, sweaty hands to pull me down beside him on the bed and then he pushed me flat on my back and removed his pants. Bile rose in my throat. The nightmare returned. Again I was pressed back into a mattress, while a monster panted and sweated on top of me. I stared at the bright orange walls, willing myself to survive. The world may as well have been a million miles away. No one could save me. When he finished he rolled off and fell asleep, while I wished for death. I washed and washed, but I knew I would never be clean.

From that day I wasn't only his maid, I was his sex slave as well. I would squeeze my eyes tight and wish to wake up from the nightmare. But of course it wasn't a dream, and each new day dawned and each new night ended in the same terrible way.

———————◆———————

On Sunday mornings Uncle would put on a fancy suit to go to church. It killed me knowing who he really was, but seeing him praise God. Now, when I see men in the church pews, I wonder if they're all like Uncle. I know God forgives, but how does he feel about Uncle selling women six days a week?

# Running

--------◆--------

Over time I was given a few liberties, such as being allowed to nip out to the shop for a moment. Once or twice I was sent out to find a woman who was lost and help her back to the flat. On those rare occasions I would stop and stare, trying to memorise the businesses and street signs, and form some understanding of my whereabouts to store for the future. I would stand in the middle of the busy sidewalks, shocked that so many people could pass by me and not see me. Surely it was obvious by looking at me that all was not well. I felt marked, but no one seemed to notice. I lacked the language and the courage to ask for help. Who would I go to? Where would I run? I believed that the police in Eastern Europe were still looking for me for attempted murder, so I did not trust them to help me. It seemed that my future was in the flat.

On the streets I would keep my eyes peeled, looking for the Eastern Europeans. I knew that they would kill me, or worse, if they found me, so I would rush back to the flat, shut the door and breathe a sigh of relief. I had evaded them again.

Occasionally I would see Andy around. He would arrive to speak with Uncle, exchanging fat wads of cash for his services. One day he seemed dishevelled. "Uncle, let's go to the kitchen to talk," he said.

"OK, my man. I am following you," said Uncle. He followed Andy, where they talked for about an hour. When they were finished Andy left straightaway and Uncle came to me. "You didn't tell me that you are in trouble with the police!" he said, with anger in his voice. I knew instantly that Andy had been in touch with the Eastern Europeans and that they hoped he would return me if he knew that I was in trouble. "I don't want the police coming here to me," he said, shaking his head. "I don't need the police on my toes. You will stay here now. Don't leave," he said. I could see that he was nervous and my fear grew.

A few hours later Andy returned. "Esther, can you help me get something out of the car?" I looked to Uncle, who nodded. I followed Andy down the stairs, fear choking me. As we approached the vehicle I could see my yellow bag in the back seat. *He is taking me back to the Eastern Europeans*, I thought. *I can't do this. I cannot do this.* My mind began to race. I knew that if I got in that car I would die. Andy was behind me. "Go on now, Esther," he said. I nodded my consent and reached for the handle. I began to open the door. Satisfied, Andy went around to the other side.

In that moment I moved with a speed and courage that I didn't know I still had. I reached over the seat to grab my bag, knowing that I needed my passport. Then I quickly jumped away from the car. Andy saw me and came around to me, but I was quicker. It was light out and the streets were busy. "Don't come near me. I will scream," I said.

"Come on now, Esther. Don't be stupid. You don't know where you are and you already have so many enemies. Get in the car. Uncle can't risk having you, so I'm just taking you somewhere safe," he said, taking another step towards me.

"Not another step," I said, meeting his eyes.

"You have nowhere to go," he said. He began to walk towards me with confidence.

It was as if I grew wings. I turned and ran with all of my might, knowing that my life depended on it. When I glanced back I saw that he was in the car following me. I ran knowing that I was being hunted. When his car was no longer in sight, I crossed the street and hid myself behind some large rubbish bins. I heaved and heaved, catching my breath, tears on my cheeks. I waited, watching the cars go past, his going slowly back and forth, until after some time he sped off. I was alone.

As I sat behind the bins my mind raced around me. Yes, I was finally free, but in a country with millions of people and I had nowhere to go. I had left behind food at least. What would I do when I grew hungry? As the last bits of cocaine and beer left my system my thoughts grew darker. My foster parents would have a laugh if they could see me now. *I've amounted to nothing but trash, as they always said I would. No one in the world truly cares about me.* People passed, no one seeing me behind the bins, even those who came close enough to throw their rubbish away. *Where is my mum? Surely she must love me a little bit? She spent nine months with me when I grew inside of her belly. Do I ever cross her mind?*

I alternated between laughing maniacally and crying hysterically. All I had was a bag full of make-up and sexy underwear – nothing to help me make it on my own. I noticed the cars whizzing past. Maybe now was the time to put myself out of my misery. If I stepped onto the street, I could end it all and no one would miss me. But I would finally be free of the pain.

And what about God? Hadn't he had enough of messing with me? In churches I had been taught that God was a God of love, but I laughed at the emptiness in that. The children's Bible I used to read portrayed him as a good guy, but that felt opposite to the truth I was living.

As the day continued, I realised that I had two choices: go back to Uncle and beg, or find someplace to go. I could see people rushing into the Tube station, and the mass of people made me think that it was a good place to hide. I didn't have an Oyster card to catch the train, or the money to buy one, but I knew how to sneak around, so I blended with the crowd and into the Underground. In the bathroom mirror I used the sink to wash up and smooth my hair so I wouldn't look a fright. I drank from the sink, as I felt dehydrated. *OK, now what?* I thought. I closed my eyes and asked again. *Where do I go from here?* Suddenly a vision of Sophia came to me. Since I arrived in the UK she was the only one who had truly seen me. I could ask her for help. That would mean that I would need to wait outside the brothel without being seen. It was risky, but it was the only thing that I could think of.

I made myself invisible that day, which was surprisingly easy. When it neared eight o'clock that night, I made my way towards the brothel. I remained in the shadows, covering my face as nonchalantly as I could. With luck, I heard Sophia's voice chatting away on her mobile phone. When I saw her I stepped onto the pavement so she could see me. She immediately hung up the phone and said, "What the hell are you doing here?" In broken English I explained where I had been and what had happened. Her face showed compassion. "Look," she said, looking over her shoulder. "We need to get out of here before somebody sees you. We'll go to my friend's place and we can chat more there."

I nodded my compliance. I was fearful about where she was taking me, but she was my only hope. What choice did I have? "Do you have a train card?" she asked.

"No," I said.

"It's OK," she answered, rummaging through her purse. "I'm sure I have a spare here." With a smile on her face, she pulled one out.

We rode the train in silence. Packed public transport didn't seem the right place to continue our conversation. We switched to a second train. I felt nervous, but more at ease the more distance was put between myself and Uncle. Finally Sophia stood, "This is our stop." We walked for what seemed like miles, the tiny homes indistinguishable.

"My friend Rico lives here. It's very tiny, but I'm sure he won't mind if you stay here for a few days while we figure out what to do." As we walked she continued to chat. "I knew something was off with you. Uncle never wanted to let you out of his sight. I'm old enough to be your mother. Someone like me knows what she's doing and is smart enough to survive this game. I get so mad when I see those pigs with young girls like you!" I nodded. "Look," she said. "I'll do what I can to help you. This is not the life for you. But after all you've been through, I'm not sure how normal your life can really be. You're just a child. It makes my blood boil."

She knocked confidently on Rico's door. When he answered she began talking quickly in Portuguese. I couldn't understand them, but I knew it was serious. They kept glancing at me.

We walked down the hall and into a tiny living room. "You want a cigarette?" she asked me.

"Yes, please," I said. It felt amazing when the smoke entered my lungs. I began to relax.

"Rico says you can stay a few days. His landlord won't let you stay on much longer than that. But tonight, let's not worry about anything! We are going to eat, drink and chat, and together we'll come up with a plan."

"OK," I said. I glanced nervously at Rico.

"Oh, don't worry, girl," he said. "I won't touch you. We might be what they call 'dirty Portuguese', but we still have our souls! Here's a beer, relax. I will get some food for you. When was the last time you ate?"

I immediately felt at ease with him. "I don't really know," I said.

He laughed. "Well, let me show you the wonders of Portuguese cuisine," he said. Rico's mannerisms and face were calming, almost boyish, and I realised that he was the first guy in ages that didn't look at me like a piece of meat.

I filled up on a delicious meal of chicken and rice, and then had a shower. When I returned to the room Sophia handed me a rolled-up note and a line. "Let's relax," she said. "We have nowhere that we need to be."

The drug hit the back of my throat and I smiled. I felt safe. I felt happy. That was a good night. We sat on the couches, drinking, smoking and chatting. We leaned up against one another like kittens, no sexual pressures lingering in the air. Rico and Sophia both told me about their lives. Rico was working as a callboy and Sophia in the brothel. Rico's mother was dying back in Portugal and the money he earned was sent home to pay for her treatments. Sophia was sending her money home to support her children. Their father was an abusive alcoholic, so she had left them with her mother and came to the UK to earn money. "If our mothers knew what we were really doing here to make money, it would break their hearts," she said. "Especially me," said Rico. "I wait for calls from desperate housewives or old gay men and then I go," he said. "That would kill her quicker than her sickness."

"Without a visa we have no choice, really," said Sophia. "Someday I will send enough money back home that I can go too."

I opened up too, crying as I told them about my life and how I had ended up there.

Sophia held me. "We got you, girl! We're going to get you out of this! There has to be something better for all of us."

The next morning Sophia had to go home, but I stayed on with Rico for a few days. We shared a small bed, but I was safe and happy. He never tried to touch me, and he fed me and cared for me.

"I have a friend named Talitha," he said. "She owns an underground strip club. I know that it's not a good job, but it's better than selling your body for sex."
I sat silently.

"I know that it's not what you want, but it could help you to save a little money," he said. "Besides," he said, "unfortunately I only know people who own brothels or strip clubs."

"OK," I agreed. "At least in the club I don't have to have sex with men."

Though I didn't have a *good* plan, I at least had a plan. We headed to Talitha's; I was high on cocaine and had my meagre belongings in a dingy backpack.

# Dancing

———— ✦ ————

It was a clandestine strip club hidden in a posh central
London office building. We entered in the daylight,
but inside the dim lighting came from blue neon lights.
Heavy black tarps covered the natural light, saving
the club from prying eyes. In the main room there was
a circle of chairs and a CD player. Rico found Talitha
quickly and introduced me, summing-up my life in
twenty seconds of Portuguese.

"Can you dance?" she asked, looking at me.

"No," I said, "but I'll figure it out." She laughed a
booming laugh.

"Let me show you around," she said, putting her arm
around my shoulder. Though her words were friendly,
I didn't trust her vibe. Still I followed. This was my new
gig, like it or not. "Here's the kitchen," she said. It was
a small room with a countertop covered with bottles
of alcohol and cocaine. "Here's the private room," she
pointed. The private room was for private dances.
There were curtains hung up to give a bit of privacy
between each dancer and customer. I would learn
later that night that dancers did have sex for money,
but it was always their choice. The thin curtains
couldn't conceal the sound of that. "It's twenty quid

for a private dance, paid upfront, and they can't touch you. They may offer you more, but that's up to you," Talitha said. "If anyone gets hands-y, just holler and one of my men will take care of it," she said.

"OK," I said shyly.

"Ha! This is no place to be shy. If you don't get aggressive, you're likely to be hungry."

"OK," I said again, more loudly.

We hung out as the other dancers arrived. Most were friendly enough, using fake names such as Claudia, Maria and Nadia, most speaking Portuguese and laughing. We shared drinks and cocaine, making the mood light.

When the men began to arrive, the dancers took turns in the middle of the circle. Each one looked far more confident than I felt. "I don't want to do that," I said to one.

"Then grab one of them flirtatiously and invite him to a private dance. Pick a short song, get your cash and move on."

I nodded, appreciating her advice. I approached a man on the side of the circle and put my hand on his arm. "Dance?" I asked. He turned to me, his eyes hungry, and nodded. I led him to the side room.

"Twenty quid up front," I said, putting out my hand. He reached into his pocket and pulled out a wad of money, handing a note to me silently. I led him to a chair and pushed him down. "No touching," I said.

I stepped back and pressed play, trying to mimic the moves that I saw the other girls doing. I removed my bra and immediately felt dirty, but I pushed the thoughts from my mind. *Dancing is better than sex. Dancing is better than sex. Dancing is better than sex.*

When the song ended, I turned immediately and walked away, covering my breasts and leaving the room. I drank and did another line, and then I did it again, and again, and again, until I had a hundred pounds. I could pay Talitha her percentage of my earnings for the night, buy the cocaine that I needed to stay high enough to survive, and pay for a place to lay my head at Talitha's place. When I had enough money, I sat in the corner, drinking and using until the night was over.

The next night I did it all again – and the next and the next. It became a pitiful existence. The dancing made me feel dirty. I looked at these men, some who seemed to have it all together, wondering why they would need to pay for the affection of a stripper. I despised the looks they gave me as I danced before them, a wolf devouring his prey. When the first wolf reached out and grabbed my breast, I screamed and Talitha's men came running. The wolf was dragged from the chair. "I said don't touch me!" I screamed.

There were regulars, men who questioned me as I sat in the corner at the end of each night. "You could make so much money with a face like that," they said. "Why aren't you up there taking command of the room?" they asked.

"I don't want to do this," I said. No one, not even the ones who would call themselves my "friend" would ask more about this – or offer to help me.

"Cheers," they would say, drinking with me. It felt like a vegetative state: I was alive, but barely there. I was drinking early in the day to work up the nerve to dance, drinking and using while I earned my money, and drinking and using when it was over to cope with the pain.

———————————— ✦ ————————————

After a few months the club needed to move the locations. This time we were in a two-storey flat. The dancing took place on the bottom floor, so the top floor would insulate the noise of the music from the flat above us. The customers always found us. It seemed that there were enough men to pay enough for every dancer every night. Every night felt the same.

The only day that stands out to me is one day when a new girl arrived. She looked so young and timid, on the arm of a Portuguese gangster wannabe. I recognised her expression as the one that I usually made. When she was alone I approached her. "Are you OK?" I asked.

"Pardon?" she asked.

"I'm just asking if you are OK. Who are you here with?"

"That's my boyfriend," she said. Though it seemed doubtful, I saw genuine affection in her eyes.

"What are you doing here?" I asked.

"Well things are a bit tough right now, so I'm going to dance to make some extra money. My boyfriend is here to protect me from the men," she said.

"Oh, OK," I said, leaving her as her boyfriend returned to the room. He looked at me harshly and I could see her shaking her head.

I approached Talitha. "How old is that girl?"

"She's sixteen," Talitha said. I felt nauseous.

"Isn't there anything we can do? She's just a baby!" I cried.

"Are you kidding me?" Talitha said, looking credulous. "Her boyfriend is a Romeo pimp. If you try to 'help' her, he's likely going to kill you."

"But Talitha . . ." I argued.

"Esther, you need to leave it alone," she said. The look on her face told me that she was serious.

She danced for two nights and I never saw her again. She still haunts my thoughts, but what was I supposed to do? I couldn't even help myself.

# Karam

Karam was part of a group of Turkish drug dealers who frequented Talitha's club from time to time. They were around at the first flat and they followed us when we moved to the two-storey flat. These men weren't our average customers, they were big time, trafficking cocaine and heroin into the country, making ten thousand, minimum, at each sale. I took notice of the wads of cash in their hands. "Who are these guys?" I asked Talitha after they returned several times in two weeks.

"You don't want to mess with them. Drug kings from Turkey," she answered seriously. The men dressed in fabulous suits, their necks and wrists dripping with gold. Even their teeth were gold-plated. They drove around in Jeeps and Range Rovers, clearing the club when they arrived. They were bigger and more powerful than Talitha's men, and when the women saw the huge wads of cash that they carried, they rushed to be the one to provide dances and attention.

Karam wore sunglasses, indoors, day or night. I would dance for him occasionally, but preferred as usual to sit and drink, numbing myself with alcohol and cocaine. One night, as I writhed before him, the light hit just so and I could see behind his glasses a huge dent where an eye should be. I think he could see that I saw, but I kept my mouth shut and walked away when the dance ended.

A few nights later Karam approached me again, offering me a drink. "You don't seem much like these other women here," he said. "Why is that?"

"What do you mean?" I asked.

"Well, all of these whores get an eyeful of our money and they are all over us. You're different. You know that you could make very good money from us, but instead you sit and drink with us," he said.

"I guess I've just seen more of life than they have," I answered. "I've already learned my lessons."

Karam smiled. "You're a clever one," he said.

Karam's visits became more frequent. He would usually request a dance from me alone and then he would sit and we would drink together. I could tell that he was interested in me and my suspicions were confirmed one night when he said, "You know that you can walk away with me and I will make your life much better. I can help you get out of this, maybe go to college and make something of yourself."

Of course, I knew that I couldn't truly trust him – he was a man. "Let me think about that," I said flirtatiously. I had learned that these men liked to be kept happy and outright denying him wouldn't have gone well. I knew that Karam was married, and most likely wanted me as his "side piece", a pretty, little trophy that he could show off while making deals.

One night, after he was finally bored of the club, he said, "let's go somewhere else to party."

I looked around at the small smoke-filled rooms and agreed. It was worth stringing Karam along just to have a change of scenery. I took Talitha aside to tell her what was happening.

"That's really good," she said. "I see that Karam treats you with a lot of favour. Make sure you bring him back to us later at the end of the night so he and his friends can come and spend some money in the club. Of course you'll get a cut," she said. I winked at her conspiratorially, though I oddly had no interest in this plan, and took Karam's arm as he offered it to me.

Karam and his mates took me with them to a nearby snooker club. There were loads of velvety green snooker tables. We sidled up to the bar and spent the night drinking, talking and playing snooker. As we settled back into a banquette Karam said, "Aren't you going to ask me about my eye?"

"It's none of my business," I answered.

"A lot of women ask me about it so that they can smother me with affection in return for my money," he said.

"Well, I'm happy to talk about it with you if you'd like," I said, "but it's obviously not an easy topic for you, so why would I bring it up?"

"I respect that. You are a clever girl indeed," he said. "I'll be back."

When he returned with drinks he turned to me. "I was racing my mate on my bike and I ended up crashing. Unfortunately, because I was a very good-looking man in my early twenties, I wasn't wearing a helmet, so my face got split in half. I lost my eye, and I have a metal plate in my head now."

"That's not what I expected," I said honestly. I'd assumed it had been some sort of drug deal gone wrong.

"It doesn't bother me when people ask about it," he said, "but the last man who *laughed* at me didn't live to see the next day."

I shrugged as if the information didn't bother me. And it truly didn't. I was still zoned out on cocaine; I hadn't felt much in a long time.

I turned to Karam. "So Talitha has a plan for your money," I said, sharing my conversation from earlier with him.

He pulled me closer and smiled. "I see that I can trust you, you clever girl!" He gestured to his mates. "We all see what she is like. Just another whore who only cares about cocaine and money."

He boasted to his mates, "Esther is different." I just smiled another fake smile. If he wanted me to be proud I could play the part.

It became a semi-habit, the walls trapping me changing from the strip club and Talitha's apartment to the snooker clubs with Karam. The nights with Karam were preferable to the strip club. He never asked for more than my conversation when we were away. In the club I would still dance for him, but we spent most of our time drinking together. I had not developed feelings for him – in my eyes he was just another man who wanted something out of me – but I preferred his company to dancing for another stranger.

After about a month Karam pulled me aside one night, looking more serious than usual.

"Look, Esther. It's no secret. You and all the others can clearly see that I have my eye on you. I do like you, and I want to help you, but at the end of the day, I can't have you here dancing for other men."

"Right," I said, not sure where he was going with it.

"I can't have another man rubbing it in my face that you danced for them. I'm ready to provide for you, somewhere to live and all of my protection. All you have to do is be good to me, and not mess around on me."

I stood unmoving, not sure what to say. *Would being kept by Karam be any better than dancing in a club? Surely in an apartment, sex would be demanded – and I don't want to have sex with Karam. But he has promised me a chance to go to school, and a real future.*

"What do you say, Esther?" he asked again.

I paused thinking about what he offered. "I'll be back in a few days. You can answer me then," he said. I nodded. I really needed to think.

———————— ✦ ————————

The next night another group of drug dealers came into the club. I was familiar with them. They always seemed angry, and I knew not to get on their bad side. Everyone smiled and nodded when they talked to them or made demands of them.

One of them grabbed me by the arm. "Talitha is out of booze. You're coming with us to pick some up," he said. I nodded and followed him to the door. He wasn't the kind of man that I could deny, not if I wanted to be safe. Every night was a new kind of risk.

Talitha swayed, drunk and high. "Hurry back," she smiled and winked.

We walked along the dimly lit hallway and down the steps to his car. I kept quiet, smiling, but not giving him the impression that I wanted more from him. I was simply here to go to the market with him. He began to talk. "How long have you known Talitha?" he asked.

"For some time now," I said, keeping it vague.

"What's her deal?" he asked.

"What do you mean?"

"She seems a little out of control. It seems that more and more she is only concerned with getting high, not with making money."

"It's none of my business, to be honest."

"I can tell that you are a very smart girl. Someone like you should be in charge. You know that we have power and money. I can get you set up in your own house or flat somewhere, and you can be in charge. We will pay the rent, protect you and pay you really well, you'll just need to get Talitha's girls to come and work for you. What do you think?"

I knew that I needed to respond very carefully. If I denied him, it would probably be the end for me. These men were powerful, and they wouldn't want Talitha to know what they were planning to do. I smiled. "Really? That's a very generous offer. Are you sure I'm the right person for the job?"

"I know you're not stupid. If there's anyone who we think could do it, it's you. Why don't I give you a couple of days to think about it? OK?"

"OK," I agreed.

When we returned to the club I saw how his eyes met those of the other men, an almost imperceptible nod passing between them. This liquor run had not been coincidental. The men bought me drink after drink and line after line. I didn't need to dance that night.

In the early morning light when the men left and we headed to sleep, I began to weigh my options. *Could I be like Talitha? It might be nice to have some control after all the turmoil that I've been through. It might be nice to call the shots.* But then I began to remember the moments that had brought me here. Each person who had owned me, used me, sold me, and I knew that I couldn't do that to another girl.

Having power and money were not worth losing my humanity.

I made up my mind. The next time Karam came into the club, I would leave with him. It was another risk, but it seemed like the best choice.

Luckily Karam returned to the club that evening. He came to me immediately. "Let's go to the garden for a cigarette."

"OK," I said. I followed him quietly, my mind racing. Once I told him yes, there would be no going back.

He lit my cigarette from his own and passed it to me. I inhaled deeply, enjoying the burn in my lungs. He looked at me seriously. "Have you thought about what I told you?"

"Yes," I answered. "Last night some men were in here, and they wanted to put me in a house and put me in charge of a bunch of girls. They want me to steal girls from Talitha. But I don't want that. I can't do that to another girl. I've decided to go with you."

He smiled. "I'm very happy to hear that, and glad that I won't have to come to this hellhole to see you anymore. And you're smart. You've made the right choice. They may have put you in charge of some girls, but they would have ultimate control over you."

"I know."

"And once again you've proven your loyalty by telling me everything. If everything stays this way, I promise to take care of you." He waited as I nodded my understanding. "We will leave in an hour. Go and get your things together, but make sure nobody notices you."

I returned to the cramped rooms inside. Everything was dark as normal. A young girl stood in the middle, disrobing as men with vacant eyes watched her. Talitha was snorting a line. She threw her head back and laughed loudly. No one even noticed me. When an hour passed I walked quietly towards the door and departed unnoticed. Karam was waiting at the bottom of the stairs.

"Let's go. I've booked you a hotel for the next couple of days while I look for a permanent place for you to stay. And don't worry. I won't be joining you in the bed. I know that you need to get some rest."

I sighed, leaning back against the headrest. The London streets passed outside the window. The clock on Karam's dashboard said 4:00 a.m. I was exhausted. *Am I making the right decision? What comes next? How is Karam going to be now that we are alone? Could he be telling me the truth – that I can go to school and leave this world behind?* I was anxious to lock the hotel door behind me and sink into a deep sleep. When I woke, I would find out.

# Hackney

Karam left me with some money and instructions to eat and rest and told me that I would see him in a few days, but I was too exhausted for anything except sleep.
I pulled the curtains closed and got under the covers. The room swirled around me. I had been high and drunk for months, and now I felt terrified as I grew sober. My heart beat far too quickly and my mouth shrivelled up with dryness. My nose was filled with dried blood from all the cocaine that I had been using.

Alone in the dark I began to hear voices. First Tomas, then Uncle, then Talitha, then my foster parents, the kids at school who didn't see my suffering. Tomas's voice was so loud that I found myself out of bed, crawling across the carpet to the peephole. *Has someone found me? Had Karam actually sold me out?*

I returned to bed, but the voices would not stop haunting me. I knew that I was alone, but I couldn't truly convince myself. I ended up on the floor, sobbing as I had never done before. I cried for everything that I had endured. I cried for the unknown future that I now faced. I cried until I was empty and asleep on the floor.

When the morning light woke me up I cracked my eyes open. I was exhausted still, so I pulled myself back to bed and under the covers again. I slept erratically until I could no longer cope without water. I dragged myself to the sink, guzzling a half-gallon of water, and then went back to bed.

When I woke again it was dark and there was a text on the phone from Karam.

"Are you OK?"

"Yes, all good here. Just catching up on sleep. Been a long time since I've been able to sleep this much."

"Just make sure that you are feeding yourself."

"OK."

I walked back to the bathroom for more water. I saw my reflection in the mirror and hated her. She was weak and worthless. Suddenly I screamed. "Aaargh! Stop looking at me!" I screeched. I ran back to the bed, falling asleep again.

When I woke I was covered in sweat. There was a new text on the phone from Karam, "Be with you in an hour." Knowing that I would soon have company, I washed my face with cool water and made myself a sugary tea. I sat sipping it at the table. I was still tired.

Karam arrived in a good mood, but his face turned when he saw the money he'd left still on the counter. "Haven't you eaten, Esther? All of the money is still here."

"I couldn't leave. I feel too horrible to go out."

"It's probably from all the partying that you've been doing." I nodded. "When was the last time you were sober?" I shrugged. "Well let me help you to the car. I've found you a place to stay at my friend's flat for a while. I'll be paying your rent. Once we get there I'll go get you some food."

"OK," I nodded. We walked to the car and travelled mostly in silence.

"Are you OK? You look pale."

"I'm just a bit hungover," I said. I couldn't wait to be out of the car.

"You've got to start taking care of yourself, or else you won't last long."

"It's not that easy being me," I answered.

"Well I'm going to help you, if you let me," he answered. "Just make sure that you don't talk to anyone. Don't tell anyone where you are. The only people who will come to see you are me and my mates."

"OK," I agreed. When we parked, a Rastafarian was outside. He held out keys to Karam, who used them to open the door to a little flat.

Karam made a sweeping movement with his arms. "This place is yours for now." A smile, so rare, formed on my face. *A place where I can be alone!* I was happy at that moment. When Karam returned with some fast-food, I could barely eat. It tasted like cardboard. "We've got to get you back to yourself. You'll do it.

Drink more water than beer and quit the nose candy,"
Karam laughed.

———————◆———————

The days passed easily, and I adjusted to a more
regular life – sleeping at night and being awake
during the day. Karam would be in and out of the flat.
He received a lot of texts on his phone, and he would
leave when he needed to do a deal. Occasionally his
friends would be around.

On one noteworthy day, Karam came into the flat
with a gift bag. "Got you something," he said, flinging
the bag to me. I looked inside. There were stacks and
stacks of cash: twenty- and fifty-pound notes. I had
never seen that much money in my life.

"I made a great deal today. But here, I feel generous,
and I want to see you in something nice. Go shopping
and get yourself some new clothes. Get a dress," he
said, holding out a wad of about five hundred pounds
to me.

"Thank you," I said.

"I have some business calls to make, but you should
go enjoy yourself. We'll go out tonight to celebrate,"
he said.

Nervously I left the flat, as I was always sure that
Tomas would find me, even though London was a city
of eight million people. I hated dresses, but Karam had
requested one, so I found a beautiful black and white

print that felt elegant. Despite the uncertainty of my new life with Karam, it was better than being with Talitha or Uncle, and I didn't want to mess things up for myself.

That night I took a shower and carefully applied a bit of make-up. Slipping on the dress I felt beautiful, and when I emerged from the room I saw on Karam's face that he was impressed. He grinned and exclaimed, "Wow! You look even better than I imagined. Come on," he said, grabbing my hand. "I want to show you off to my mates. They're going to be so jealous."

We went back to the old snooker club where we used to hang out. The drinks were flowing, and I noticed immediately how much more politely his mates were treating me. I guess I had reached a new level of respect now that I was by Karam's side and wasn't at that dungeon of Talitha's. I tried to smile and be happy that I was safe, but I still felt a darkness in my soul.

# Lessons from Karam

Living with Karam felt like a battle of the soul. I saw him as a ticket out of Talitha's, but I also knew that he had feelings for me and living with him meant that I was immersed in a life of drugs in a whole new way.

The first time he wrapped his hands around me and pulled me into him I fought back nausea. "You know how much I like you, Esther. I have been dreaming about getting you into my bed," he said. I trembled, but it wasn't from anticipation, it was from fear. As he moved his hands around I tried to go away into my head like I used to in the brothel. I knew that if I left him I would be returning to a dark underworld and that I would be trading one body for many men.

I hated every minute of it, but it seemed like the safest choice.

I noticed many things about Karam's life. He was in a different car, a good car, but nothing too flashy. "One mistake a lot of young dealers make is buying too much too soon," he explained. "They attract attention when they make them wonder, 'What in the world is an eighteen-year-old doing with that kind of car and clothing?'" He always talked to me as if he was teaching me. "I also don't want people to be able to track me back to my house," he added. "I know I'm not eighteen anymore, but I don't want the extra attention from the wrong people. Got to be smart."

He often used a part of the flat as a drug lab. He and his mates would bring in bags of flat packages full of cocaine and heroin, cover the flat in plastic and then cut the drugs with other substances. The street dealers would never know the difference and Karam and his mates would profit even more.

He often took me with him to make deliveries. I think this benefited him in two ways: he was able to show me off to his mates, and I would make him seem more innocent if he were ever pulled over by the police. "If the police pull me over I will just say that I'm out on a drive with my daughter," he laughed. My stomach turned at that comment. *How long can I survive this? I may be freer than I was at Talitha's, but I'm still in a prison. Why must all of my life be lived for another person's plans?*

He also trained me to do deliveries. "Take this backpack and get on the train. Exit at Camden Avenue and make the drop," he said. He handed me a bag full of heroin.

"But what if something happens to me?" I asked.

"It won't. I will have eyes on you the entire time. If there is any danger you'll be taken care of."

"OK," I said. I knew that the drugs and the backpack full of cash I would be trading it for were the real motivators, but that he liked claiming me as his own as well. Doing the drop was like a test. Would I do a runner if I had forty thousand pounds in my hands? Even if I were brave enough to run, where would I go? Could I outrun those he had sent to follow me? I doubted it.

When he drank he often became possessive of me, ranting about his power over me.

"Do you ever think about running away from me?" he would ask.

"No," I lied.

"Don't even think about it, Esther. I have eyes everywhere. Everywhere. If you tried to leave, you would be returned within twenty-four hours." He took another drink and peered at me. "What about the money? You ever think about taking the money?"

"Of course not," I lied again.

"You better not," he warned again. "I have eyes everywhere. I won't have you making me look like a fool if you end up with some other man or woman." He often reminded me that I was alone and powerless, that there were multiple people that I had crossed, and that the police would never believe or care about a girl like me. I believed him. I had been passed from one person to the next, never really making my own decisions, and though I dreamed of being free, I didn't see how it could ever happen.

There are moments from that time that haunt me to this day.

One day a new shipment of heroin was delivered. "Call up one of the lab rats," Karam said to his mate. His friend quickly made a call on his phone, laughing to himself.

"What is a lab rat?" I asked.

"Some trash. Someone that we can test the product on," Karam said, emotionless. He went on to explain that they needed an addict to test their product. If the heroin was weak, the person wouldn't have any effect at all, because it was already in their system. If the product was good, they would see it in the lab rat.

His friend came in with a woman. She was in her mid-forties, with long, unbrushed brunette hair. She seemed nervous. I saw a beautiful gentle soul, but one that was covered by the scratches and pockmarks of an addict. We all knew that she would do anything for another hit.

I sat in the back of the room and watched as she put the needle into her arm and pushed down on the syringe. It was as if she were struck by lightning. She dropped to the floor immediately, foaming at the mouth, with her legs spasming behind her. Karam and his mates jumped up and cheered, laughing and clapping each other on the back. I was horrified, dropping my head down as I fought back vomit rising in my throat.

"It's pure," said Karam. "Put her in the back room," he said to his mate. The woman was clearly overdosed, but they were happy about the product they had scored. He came to me.

"You don't need to think about her. She's just worthless scum off the street."

I was scared. I saw the power they had. I wish I had known that I could go to the police, but I was nineteen and I was afraid. I had no power. So I stayed and continued to play the role I was assigned, but when I looked in the mirror, I was disgusted by myself.

# Black Hole

My life as Karam's doll left me constantly feeling like I was in a black hole. The days were for sleeping, and the nights were for drugs and alcohol. I began to miss Talitha's.

"Can you take me to Talitha's?" I asked Karam.

"What the hell do you want to go there for?"

"She's my friend," I said.

"That whore is a lot of things, but she's not your friend," Karam argued.

I guess I missed the mania of being at the club. At Karam's I was alone with my thoughts, which turned darker and darker. I hated who I had become. I felt like a split personality: one girl who desperately wanted to die, and another who wanted nothing other than being high.

Karam took me to clubs but would then accuse me of being with other men. "You're always with me," I argued. "When do you think this is happening?"

"You better be loyal to me," he would warn. Then one night he said the unthinkable, "I want you to have a baby with me." My head spun quickly towards him, questioning if I was hearing his words correctly.

My first response was to laugh in his face. "A baby?! Why the hell would I want a baby?"

"I think you would be an amazing mother," he said. "And maybe that would keep you from going out and drowning yourself with booze."

"There is no way I would ever bring a baby into this hellhole!" I screamed. "Wake up and look around! I have nothing to give a baby. I won't make the same mistakes my mother did."

Karam hated my answer, skulking around the flat, commenting on my drug and alcohol use, yet never keeping them from me. I partied as much as possible, trying to draw closer to the girls in the club.

Karam had promised me a life of independence, but so far I had only been kept. He wouldn't allow me to get a bank account and grew angry on several occasions when I mentioned getting a job. "There are still too many people looking for you. You need to stay with me so that you'll be safe," he said. When I mentioned that I wanted to apply for a job I had seen advertised, he exploded. "What the hell do you need a job for? I have everything you need! I buy your food, your drugs and give you a place to live. I have what you need."

I was in another powerless situation and found myself cutting again. It started one night when I was alone in the flat. I heard voices in my head, sinister whispers about my worthlessness. I remembered my foster parents, and my mother, and Carmen, and Sonia, and Tomas, and Uncle, and Talitha, and every man that had forced himself inside me. I remembered that I would continue to be used by Karam. I remembered that many of my old schoolmates were at university, or living clean and happy lives – and I wondered if any of them remembered me.

I dismantled a razor and held it against my arm. I made a small movement, drawing blood and a deep breath. Temporarily I would forget the pain of my life and let the sadness drip from my arm.

It became a habit. On my nights alone, I would drown myself in alcohol, cut open my arm and cry, sad music blaring from the stereo. I would lie down on the floor or couch and howl like a dog, releasing my pain into the arm. I pictured my death, wishing I had the nerve to do it, but always too afraid to follow through. I imagined what it would be like to make a noose and step off a chair, waiting for death to take me, but I was always too afraid for those waiting moments. Still I longed for peace and escape. For now, the best I could do was to remain drunk and high.

# The End of Karam

One of the dancers at Talitha's needed a safe space to stay, so I offered her a room in the flat with Karam and me. Her company would be welcome for my loneliness, though she herself was wounded.

She was in the upstairs room and I was downstairs with Karam, who was drinking heavily.

He turned to me in anger. "You're drinking too much and all of the time," he said. "And I want you to have a baby." I stared at him blankly, refusing to engage in this conversation again. "I control you," he continued. "Without me you have nothing. The least you can do is return the favour."

He walked towards me, reaching out and placing his hands on the side of my head. He leaned in as if to kiss me, and suddenly it was as if something broke inside of me and the cage that was holding back an animal shattered like dust. I screamed and shoved him away from me.

"I am not your property!" I howled.

Shock shadowed his face and his lips curled in a snarl. "What are you going to do?"

"Esther," I heard from upstairs, "is everything OK?"

"I'm fine," I yelled, "but please stay in your room." I saw rage cross Karam's face, and I worried for my friend upstairs. I didn't know what to do. Without thinking I raced to the kitchen and grabbed a knife from the block on the counter. I brandished it towards him.

"What is this?" he asked. He spoke calmly, but I saw the evil in his eyes. "Where is this coming from? Think about what you're doing, girl."

Karam moved towards me and my life went in slow motion. *I could kill him and run.* Even in that moment the thought of becoming a murderer turned my stomach. Without awareness I quickly turned the knife to myself. My right hand pushed it against my arm with all of the force I had, and I slowly dragged it back.

My head burst with a light of pain that I had never felt before. Blood poured out of me, splashing against the wall. I sank to my knees and fell backwards. *Did I do it? Was I finally brave enough to end it?* I suddenly remembered my friend and screamed out, "Get out of here. Go somewhere that you will be safe." I saw the shock and disgust on Karam's face and then things went black.

I heard Karam's voice getting closer. "Now you've done it, you stupid, stupid girl," he yelled. I opened my eyes briefly and saw him pull his bottle of Jack Daniels closer. He lifted the bottle and poured it over the gash in my arm. I screamed. "Shut up, or I will end you myself," he threatened. I saw panic in his eyes. He pushed down on the wound. I don't know if he was trying to hurt me or stop the blood, but either way the pain was unbearable and the world went dark.

When I came to I saw Karam sitting, gulping from his bottle and talking to himself. *Is this going to be the pathetic end to my pathetic life? Bleeding out onto this dirty carpet in this dirty flat?* My eyes fluttered, but I kept my eyes on him. *At least it's almost over. Peace is coming.* I closed my eyes and succumbed to the dark.

———————— ✦ ————————

There was a bright light and the sound of my name being called by a voice I did not recognise. "Esther. Esther. Can you hear me, Esther?" I struggled in the dark to open my eyes and match the voice to a face. When I was able to open them enough I saw a female paramedic leaning over me. *Who in the world called an ambulance? Karam would never call an ambulance. Did a neighbour hear me scream? Where is Karam?* I looked beyond the paramedic to see Karam seated on the couch with a police officer, his head in his hands.

I looked back to the paramedic and said the word I had been too afraid to say before, "Help." No sound came from my throat, so the paramedic leaned closer.

"Talk to me, Esther," she said, looking into my eyes.

"Help," I said again. I looked directly at Karam, fear and desperation clearly visible on my face. "Help me," I said.

Her face changed instantly. "Get her to the ambulance!" she yelled. Bodies bustled around me, strapping me to the board and shuffling me towards the door of the flat. I saw her walk across the room and whisper into the ear of one of the police officers before catching up with me at the door.

I winced as I was helped down the stairs and then lifted into the back of a waiting ambulance. The blue lights flashed, bringing memories of my nights in the club, my time in the hospital at my foster parents' house, the innumerable darknesses that I had endured.

The paramedic leaned over again. "It's OK, love," she said. "You're in safe hands now. All will be OK." I watched the ambulance doors until they closed, and then shut my eyes as we sped from the kerb and away from Karam.

# Dover

I watched out of the ambulance window as we sped to the hospital. The officer never left my side as the doctors examined me and stitched up my arm. It took hours for me to sober up and for the doctors to clear me to leave the hospital. The officer waited patiently, talking very little. We drove from the hospital to the police station. I was too afraid to ask what would happen to me. Would I be in trouble? Would they find out about the gun in Eastern Europe? Would I be charged for prostitution? The officer led me to a small room with a table and two chairs. "Someone will be here with you shortly, Esther," she said kindly, shutting the door behind her. When she left, I erupted with tears. The release of the tears brought me some relief. I felt relieved that I would finally be able to share my story, but was also afraid that I wouldn't be believed. From my foster parents through to Karam, I had been warned that the police would not care about me.

After some time a different woman popped in with a glass of water. "Don't worry. Someone will be here with you soon," she said. She passed me a box of tissues and offered me a sympathetic smile. I waited longer, having no tears left.

When another police officer arrived, he said they were moving me. "We don't think it's safe for you in London," he said. I followed him down the hallway and out the back of the station. An unmarked car was waiting for me and I was escorted to the door. There was another officer in the back, who nodded at me.

I watched the lights through the window, eventually falling asleep as the car rocked me.

When I awoke, I didn't know how much time had passed. A sign out the window read "Welcome to Dover". Another new place was waiting for me.

We pulled up to a hotel. "What are we doing here?" I asked, trying to keep panic from my voice.

"We use half of this hotel to help refugees. Wait right here," the officer said. He left the car, returning ten minutes later with a room key. He escorted me to the second floor, unlocking the door and checking inside before allowing me in. "Someone will be here to help you in the morning," he said. Then he was gone. I looked around. I was alone, and though I had no clue as to what was going on, I felt safe enough. I could hear feet and voices in the hallway, so I double-checked the locks. I paced the room, expecting to see someone each time I looked through the peephole. I saw my reflection in the mirror, looking sick and broken. *Can I trust the police? Can I trust this place? Should I run? Where could I possibly go?*

I was exhausted, so I lay on the bed, pulling the covers over me, but I left my coat and shoes on in case I needed to run. I slept uneasily, waking at each ringing of the elevator. In the morning a soft knock on the door woke me. When I looked through the peephole I saw a blonde woman holding a thin file. She smiled and mouthed my name.

"Who is it?" I asked.

"My name is Anne. I've been sent by the police to help you," she said. I timidly opened the door. She smiled a bit bigger and held out her hand. "Let's sit," she said.

I sat on the chair and she on the edge of the bed while she explained that she worked for a charity that helped people like me. I didn't ask her to clarify who "people like me" were.

"The police will be coming to question you but, in the meantime, we have to find you a safe place to stay. We need something secure, away from the bad people who might want to hurt you, but it can't be here, this is just a halfway house."

I nodded, even though she was talking quickly and my head was spinning.

"We'd be happy to book you a ticket back to Eastern Europe so that you can be with your family," she said.

I scoffed, "I have no family. My foster parents would only laugh and berate me if they knew what I'd been through."

Anne looked thoughtful. "What about your parents?"

"I don't even know if my mother is alive," I said. "And if I go back to Eastern Europe, the people who got me into this mess will find me. There is only death waiting for me in Eastern Europe."

Anne nodded her head. "OK, then it's best if I find a place for you here." I began crying again in relief. Anne spoke again, "I will find you a safe place here in the UK. I'll come back tomorrow with some food, some clothes for you and some ideas about where you might go. Do you have a preferred area?"

"Just far away from London," I said. She left and I locked the door behind her again.

Exhausted, I crawled back into bed.

Anne returned the next day with a couple of bags for me. She passed me the toiletries and said that she would return in an hour so we could talk.

The shower felt amazing. I was almost in a surreal situation. It seemed that I might have finally made it to safety. Thoughts of Tomas, Uncle, Andy, Talitha, Karam and the others filled my head, but I tried to wash them off with the blood and grime. I tried to wash away the pain and confusion of the last year.

When Anne returned, she noticed the bandages on my arm, now in disarray, and promised to take me to a nurse to get the bandages repaired. She pulled some leaflets from her bag and handed them to me. "Look at these," she said. I took them from her and began to flick through them. They were glossy and they held promises of safety. Anne separated one that said "Sanctuary Haven" from the stack and said, "Sanctuary Haven. They sometimes use horses to help people deal with trauma." My face grew bright at the mention of horses. Though I had never had a pet, I had always adored animals. "Are you interested in that?"

"Yes," I answered quickly.

"OK," said Anne. "I will call them and see if they have an opening. I'll be back soon." When she left, I locked the door and made myself something to eat from the bag of food she had left.

The next day Anne returned a final time to tell me that I would be heading to Sanctuary Haven.

We walked a short distance to a train station where she purchased two tickets.

The train ride took a couple of hours, the endless hills out the window battling to bring me peace. When the conductor announced that my stop was the next stop, my heart jumped in my chest.

A woman was waiting for us on the platform. "I'm Linda," she said warmly. Though her face was friendly, I had learned to distrust everyone, so I wasn't sure if I should trust her. "I'm just a volunteer for Sanctuary Haven, but I'm here to get you there safely." She had a very happy energy, but it made me nervous. I had come this far and had no choice but to keep going.

# Sanctuary Haven

Sanctuary Haven wasn't far from the station. It was a pretty house with a gate around the yard. There were a few other women there, all of whom looked nervous, and I realised that they must be women like me. Linda walked me into an office and motioned for me to sit in a chair.

"Let's go over the house rules," she said. She began to read through a long list, stating things like staying at the property the first week, not drinking alcohol, attending church on Sundays, not sharing our personal stories with the others, but her voice changed when she said, "But most importantly, you can never ever tell anyone where you are or what your address is here."

I almost laughed, "I assure you, sharing my location is the last thing that I want to do." She seemed satisfied.

"Let me show you to your room," she said. Linda walked me upstairs to a bright and airy room. The bed was freshly made, there was a Bible next to the bed and there were a few chocolates on a side table. I smiled. "You have some time to rest and settle in. We have church in a few hours," she said.

Going to church was the last thing I wanted to do; it reminded me of that hypocrite, Uncle, but I understood that I could not stay alone, and as the new girl I didn't want to make any waves.

Linda drove me and another woman to a large warehouse a few hours later. There were bright lights and lots of smiling women in soft dresses. I felt so out of place in a bloody bandage, face red from days of tears and wearing yesterday's clothes. The women all greeted me kindly. I felt so lost that I could barely understand what was happening. They all seemed so healthy and happy. But even though they treated me with nothing but kindness, I just didn't see how I could ever fit in.

When we returned to the house I slipped into a pair of pyjamas. I pulled back the sheets and climbed into bed. The sheets were crisp and smelled clean. I closed my eyes and considered my circumstances. There was a house full of women and a guard at the door. I felt safe enough to fall asleep quickly, for the first time in years.

# Another New Normal

———— ✦ ————

I began my new life at Sanctuary Haven. Though I was away from Tomas and all those who had controlled me, I never felt in control of myself. I never felt fully safe. The weeks passed in a regular sort of routine, but it always felt like chaos. I would go to church, do work-hours at the church, meet with counsellors and talk to the police about my experience. Those days with the police were long and draining. Though I knew that they were there to help me, I always felt ashamed of the information that I needed to share. No amount of showers could make me feel clean.

It had been decided that to go after all of my perpetrators would be too much, so the police were focusing their energies on building a case against Tomas. Reliving the nightmare was often only endurable by coping with a bottle of cheap and forbidden wine.

At the safe house we were given about forty pounds a week. We would use it to buy our bus pass to the church centre, where we were expected to attend services and do work-hours. We would work in the café or the kids' centre, or clean the building. The eight pounds I spent on cigarettes felt more than necessary. At night we would gather in the courtyard, smoking to settle our hearts and, when the staff weren't nearby, sharing our pasts and hopes for the future. The other women remembered their families and kids, but when talk turned in that direction I remained silent. There was no one waiting for me on the other side of this. I tried to keep five pounds for emergency purposes, so the remainder of my meagre funds was used to buy food for the week: cheap noodles and potatoes to sustain me, and the cheapest wine I could find to help me cope.

Sanctuary Haven was in a poor part of town, in the council estates. There was a lot of shouting and loud living. The fireworks that went off each evening reminded us of gunshots, keeping us constantly in a state of unease. The thugs in the neighbourhood reminded me too much of those who had controlled my life over the last year. The nicotine in each precious cigarette and the wine that I was not supposed to have were the only things that could give me a moment of rest.

Many of the volunteers at Sanctuary Haven were from the church. They would talk with us or invite us on walks. They were there to make us feel more normal and offer us friendship. It was hard for me to open up to people, but Patricia was special.

"Hello, Chicken," she fondly nicknamed me in her strong Yorkshire accent. She always had a bright smile and her genuine heart was easy for me to see.

"You want to go to the park for a bit, Chicken?" she would ask me after I met with the police. "Let's go to the farm for a few hours, Chicken," she would say when I woke up sadder than usual. Recording video evidence for the police drained me, and Patricia was there. I will never forget the warmth that Patricia showed me, because although the purpose of Sanctuary Haven was to pull me out, the darkness always seemed to chase me.

# God

---◆---

Church was an odd place to me. Beginning with my first service at Sanctuary Haven, where everyone wore a shiny smile and a floral dress, it just seemed too good to be true. I wanted to believe that the people greeting me were genuine, but it was impossible to feel accepted and loved. *Who are these happy people? Surely people can't always feel this way?* My head swirled as I watched their bright faces, their arms lifted and eyes closed as they worshipped the Lord that they loved. *This is creepy*, I felt.

The music played and the voices lifted around me. With the first chords of the guitar and piano, my body filled with emotion. "Break every chain! Break every chain!" The voices sang around me. My body exploded with feeling and warmth. I heard about the power in the name of Jesus and physically felt chains of darkness breaking from me. Tears streamed down my cheeks and I felt warm and happy and free. I remembered the house with Rita and the loud playing of "Don't Stop Believing" and how I wanted to live. Patricia held my hand, smiling. I looked to my right and left and saw the other women like me who had literally been in bondage and were now free, and I became overwhelmed with gratitude and joy. *We are free. God has saved us. We are free. This is a miracle.* I talked to God. "Why did you save me? Why did you keep me alive? What was this all for?" With every tear I felt as if the pain was truly leaving my body. What had started as doubt had turned into belief. I was loved.

Love is a crazy emotion. I had never felt true love before, and sitting in that pew and receiving it from above was overwhelming. My body radiated joy and I battled to accept it, the love being so foreign to me.

After the service I tried to describe the feelings that had come over me to Patricia and the other ladies. "That was the Holy Spirit, Chicken," Patricia assured me. Linda, the kind volunteer from my first day, was there as well, echoing the assuredness of Patricia.

"The Holy Spirit was there with you," she said smiling. I wanted to believe. I wanted to be at peace. But as we returned to Sanctuary Haven, I wondered if it was all too good to be true.

---

Darkness was never far from me. And although I had felt peace during that moment, and thought the fear had left me and I had felt God with me, the peace was not permanent. *If God is real, why would he allow me to be raped and tortured? If God is love, why would he allow me to endure such evil? If my life has happened to me in such a tragic manner – and to so many others like me – how could God be real?*

My time at Sanctuary Haven couldn't last forever. The space was limited and, sadly, there were always new girls getting rescued and needing a place to stay. When I was told that my funding had run out, I immediately shut down, feeling cast aside once again. Patricia and Linda were there for me, assuring me of their permanency in my life. "It's going to be OK, Chicken. We're going to help you," said Patricia.

"We'll still be here for you," said Linda. Their faces were earnest, but the darkness was more powerful. I couldn't believe them.

I took the few pounds that I had and went to buy the cheapest bottle of wine I could find. I walked and walked, coming to a bridge that overlooked a parkway. I sat and drank. The darkness fell on the city and my personal darkness followed me.

*Patricia and Linda are too good to be true. They won't be around when you aren't at Sanctuary Haven. You have nowhere to go. Tomas, Uncle, Karam and the others are still out there. You will never be safe. Remember how it used to feel by releasing the pain on your arm? Do that again.*

My vision blurred as I got drunk, and the lights of the city looked beautiful. I didn't truly want to die, I had come too far, but the devil seemed to haunt me. He whispered into my ear how sweet the release of death would be. I was terrified to leave Sanctuary Haven, but death didn't scare me.

As curfew fell my phone began to ring. Patricia was calling. I silenced the phone and continued to drink. Linda called next and then Patricia again. Then they began to text. My phone was ringing in the darkness, over and over. I read the texts, which only showed love, not anger. When the phone rang again I wanted to smash it, but the best part of me ached for a real connection to someone who cared about me.

"Hello?"

"What's going on, Chicken?"

"Nothing," I slurred. I mumbled nonsense.

"C'mon on now, Chicken. Linda and I are really worried about you. Come on back so we can talk." *Damn it, they clearly know that I've gone off on one.*

"Not sure I want to return. I don't think I can keep going," I answered truthfully.

"C'mon love. That isn't true. We are here for you. We aren't going to leave you, even when you leave this house. Come on back so we can help you."

"I can't," I slurred.

"Just tell us where you are. We'll come get you." They continued to talk, but I put the phone down and began to cry. I took deep breaths. *What do I truly want to do?*

*They don't really care,* whispered the demons.

*You'll never be OK,* whispered the darkness.

*You'll never belong to someone*, whispered death.

*Love*, whispered hope.

———————◆———————

My phone rang with a text from Patricia: "Come back, Esther. Let us help you. We love you. We know that your pain feels unbearable, and it's because you've been through hell. We will not give up on you. Just come back."

I broke open and remembered God.

With a small ounce of sanity, I stood and stumbled through the park. I saw the lights of Sanctuary Haven. *What kind of trouble will I be in for missing curfew and drinking?* The door flung open and Patricia and Linda ran out, wrapping their arms around me. I burst into tears. I had expected shouting and anger and dire consequences, but I was being met with love.

They held me tight as I cried it all out, and eventually broke to say, "Let's get you a cup of tea." We sat at the little round table. I sipped the tea and tried to put my pain and fear into words. They watched me intently, nodding in understanding. I felt seen, heard, known and loved.

"Let's get you to bed," Patricia finally said. I couldn't believe that I hadn't been punished.

*Maybe that comes in the morning?* I thought to myself.

After a restless sleep, I woke and headed to the kitchen. Patricia and Linda were still there, smiling. "How's your head?" they joked. I couldn't believe that I was being met with smiles.

"What's going to happen?" I asked.

"Well, we do have to inform people about the drinking and the curfew, but our priority here is to keep you safe and healthy. We need to look after your mental health. We think you need to see a doctor."

I nodded, wanting to be compliant, but I expected the worst. "What, so they can lock me up in a psych ward?"

"No, we don't think you're crazy, but it's obvious that you need some help. You're probably depressed, you've suffered through tremendous horrors and maybe they can give you some medication to help you cope."

I told them about my experience with doctors and my foster parents, and how I had been drugged into silence. I didn't want to be a zombie again. "It's not like that here in the UK," they assured me. "We all only want to help you." They reached across the table to hold my trembling hands. "You have to trust us here, Chicken."

I closed my eyes and tried to clear my head. My foster parents were there, mocking me. Carmen was there, choosing another. Sonia was there, betraying me. Tomas was there, destroying me. Uncle was there, using me. Karam was there, owning me. My mother was there, abandoning me.

I shook my head slowly, as if to clear them all from my mind.

I was there, still living. God was there, offering hope. Patricia and Linda held my hands.

"You can do this, Chicken. Wipe your tears. You can do this."

"OK," I said finally. "I want help." I guess I realised that I had nothing to lose. Seeing a doctor, relying on the kindness of others and making a way for myself would be the only way forward.

My life had been a thick and wild forest, overgrown and full of beasts and brambles. But shining through the woods was the slightest glimmer of life. I chose to walk out of the darkness and towards the light.

# Choosing Life

In 2021 they finally caught him. It took the police two years to track him down as he was making sure he stayed off grid. Having to go through days of giving evidence to the police, talking about all that happened, was traumatising in itself but at the actual court hearing I had to sit facing the jury whilst everyone in court watched my video. It was dehumanising. I thought, *These people know every single detail of what happened,* and I was so scared of the judgement they were going to make. I knew in my heart I needed this justice but having to prove what happened to me was so, so difficult. In my head I kept hearing his voice telling me, "No one will ever believe you! You are to blame for this! It's your own fault. You will be the one who will be going to jail for what you have done!"

A few times I just wanted to quit, run away and never look back. But this was my only chance – either I do this now or I would live for the rest of my life thinking, *What if?* Just what if I could have got some justice?

The process felt like it took months. After four days in court the jury went to consider their verdict and I had to go home and wait for the outcome. Because it was

Friday I had to wait until Monday to know what they had decided. I felt so much fear and worry. I wasn't able to eat or sleep and kept crying. Finally, Monday morning I had a call and the police woman who was working with me said, "Do you want the good news?"

"Yes!" I said.

The jury found him guilty on all counts and he was going to prison for sixteen years. I fell on my sofa and I couldn't understand the feeling I was experiencing! Finally! Finally, I was listened to! He will rot in jail and, with all my being, I just hoped he'd get the treatment he deserves in jail!

———— ✦ ————

This victory was bitter sweet. Was sixteen years enough? To me personally, no way. I wanted him to rot there for the rest of his days. I wanted him to feel the pain he subjected me to. I wanted him to know what it felt like to have your soul ripped out from you and be made to feel just so small and ugly.

In the coming years I kept living with his shadow haunting me wherever I went. I could see him at night. I could see his horrible face and still felt him, and all those other men, on my skin. I felt so disgusting and I just wanted to wash that feeling off me but, whatever I did, I just could not get rid of it.

I turned to alcohol for help to numb the feelings and quiet the noises in my head, *I am just a piece of worthless rubbish. How could anyone ever want to love me or be my friend?* I have all that nastiness imprinted on me. I would cry and my soul and my body was in so much pain. I used to cry out into the night, begging for all this to stop. The pain and memories were just too much. I needed some release, and then I would self-harm. With each cut I felt release. Blood would drip down my body and it would feel like the pain from the cut was almost blocking out all the other pain. I spent many years running from these emotions and memories but running did not got me anywhere. I just kept going in circles ending up in my bedroom with bottles around me and bloody blades on the floor. Then I went back to cocaine and I thought it was the best thing. As soon as I would do it my brain would just let go and for few moments I had no care in the world. I did not care about what happened and I thought nothing and no one can touch me.

But addiction was just as crumbling as that past trauma. I would end up going out and making friends with random people or stay at some stranger's house, talking about my past without even realising how much danger I was putting myself in. Anyone listening to my weaknesses could have done whatever they wanted with me, but I just wanted someone to understand my pain or even explain to me what was happening in my head.

The good people in my life would soon leave but how could I ever blame them? There was no talk about hope or telling me that there was more for me. I lost so many beautiful people in my life because I chose addiction.

I thought that no one would ever understand how I felt or what the past had done to me.

I pushed people away who wanted to help me and thought, *I can do life on my own!*

It wasn't until this one night when I was on the verge of losing my home and when my head was telling me *You're not worthy!* that I cried out like I have never cried out before and actually spoke to God and asked him, "Please help me! I do not want to go down this road of chaos and destruction. I am sure there is more."

It took some time for me to realise that God wasn't going to just answer my prayer by changing everything immediately, but he did put things in my path to change my life.

I started to attend church more often, where people would greet me with smiling faces and ask, "How are you?" When I just quickly answered, "Yeah, I'm fine," they would say, "No, how are you really?" And that made me realise that this was a safe space to open up and a healthy environment for me to be in. When I spoke, people would listen to me and pray with me.

Worship music played and even though the first thing I wanted to do was run away and hide from all the feelings it was bringing up, I stayed and it almost felt like God himself placed his hand on my heart and said, "It's OK. Let it all out." Years of pain and fear were lifting off my chest each time I listened to worship music. I stayed and let God be in control.

Slowly I was able to appreciate each day. Instead of choosing to ignore the world around me and take the easy option of staying in bed and hiding, I would put on my headphones, listen to worship music and go for a walk. Walking with God in your heart makes you realise how many beautiful things we are given to enjoy. I love going for a walk on the beach. It's as if each time I see the sun shining on the waves I learn how to feel free and alive again.

Don't get me wrong – living with this sort of trauma will never be easy. I still have days where certain flashbacks will blow me back to those dark places, but it's how I deal with it now that matters. Yes, it's OK to mess up – we are human after all. Every day is a lesson and we keep learning until the day we die, but stand up, pick yourself up and, even when you feel pain, get out of bed, put on some good music and cry if you want. Crying will allow you to let out whatever pain you feel right there and then, and go for a walk!

Do not let the shadows of those who hurt you catch you in their grip! You are free. Breathe and look around you – the sky, the sea, feel the sand beneath your feet, breathe in life. Life is so worth living. There is beauty and a purpose for you!

# Epilogue

————— ✦ —————

I was nineteen years old when I was taken in the ambulance, away from Karam. It had been a year since I had arrived in England, desperate to start a new life, but it felt like decades.

I worked closely with the police as they built a case to prosecute Tomas. When it was time to go to court I was terrified. I sat in the same room as Tomas, but for security purposes I wasn't required to show my face. I was able to speak out and share my story from behind the safety of a screen. In the end Tomas was sentenced to sixteen years in prison. That wasn't even one year for every time that I was raped, but it was something.

Fighting in court was not easy. But I am so, so grateful that I did it. Though all of my perpetrators had warned me to avoid the police – that no one would believe me and that no one would help me – I learned that they were wrong. The police did help me through every step of the legal process and Tomas was put into prison for a very long time. It gave me a small sense of justice.

I am so grateful for the help that I received at Sanctuary Haven, for the good people who never gave up on me. I learned that there are people who truly care and who can make a difference in another person's life. I will never be able to forget the horrors that I endured, but I will never forget the love that I found in church that day and that has continually been extended to me.

Every day is a new day. Unfortunately my story doesn't end with "happily ever after". I battle darkness constantly, but I am eager to make a new life for myself. I have fallen in love with photography and animals. I have made friendships that are safe and healthy. I journal and I pray.

And I'm sharing my story with you.

If you are a victim, I encourage you to seek help. Trust in others. Go to the police and seek justice for what you have endured. Share your story.

If you are not a victim, I encourage you to extend help: volunteer, donate, pray. I could never have chosen life without the help that I received at Sanctuary Haven and from the good people at church who continued to love me. Love matters.

Though I was born no one's child, I have learned that I am someone's child. God's child.

# Last Night

Last night it felt as if the scars opened up.
Deep cuts oozing with blood.
The pain not in my body, but in my heart.

The devil was there,
Showing me a book of memories.
If I were gone no one would miss me.
I watched as the world lived on,
Each of their laughs cutting me more deeply.

Wake from this nightmare!
It's all in the past . . .
But the shadows loom large,
And it's hard to breathe.
I try to run, but my legs are stuck in place.

Then the day dawns
Sun breaking through the shadows
And I turn my eyes back to the Light.
I am not drowning.
I don't have to fight.
I can breathe again.
I am free.

# Resources

---◆---

## What to do if you believe you see someone who is being trafficked:

- If you see something, say something. Look for the signs that a person is being trafficked. In the UK you can contact the Modern Slavery and Exploitation Helpline by texting "HELP" to 21400. You can also call for free and confidentially on 08000 121 700. In the US contact the National Human Trafficking Hotline on 1-888-373-7888 or text 233733.

- Some signs of human trafficking are:

  1. A person avoids eye contact, is fearful, anxious, depressed, tense, nervous or paranoid.

  2. Poor physical health, appears malnourished, shows signs of physical and/or sexual abuse.

  3. Lack of control: has few or no personal possessions. Not in control of their own money or identification documents.

  4. Evidence of controlling relationships, not allowed or able to speak for themselves.

  5. A third party may insist on being in control of schedules or social interactions.

6. Lack of knowledge of whereabouts. Loss of sense of time.

7. Unexplained or conflicting stories.

8. Not free to come and go as they wish. (humantraffickinghotline.org)

————————◆————————

## To learn about understanding trauma:

- ACE's study Dr Nadine Burk Harris

- Trust-based relational interventions Dr Karyn Purvis

- Book: *The Body Keeps the Score* by Dr Bessel van der Kolk

————————◆————————

## Brave Global resources:

Brave In Real Life Book

Brave Interactive Journals

————————◆————————

## Resources for victims and survivors:

*Comprehensive list of resources in the US:*

https://www.acf.hhs.gov/sites/default/files/
documents/orr/traffickingservices_0.pdf

https://ojjdp.ojp.gov/programs/human-trafficking-resources

https://www.missingkids.org/HOME

https://humantraffickinghotline.org/

https://polarisproject.org/

https://www.unicefusa.org/mission/protect/trafficking

https://exoduscry.com/

*Other U.S. resources:*

https://www.castla.org/about/

https://freedomnetworkusa.org/

https://fairgirls.org/our-mission/

https://thecupcakegirls.org/

https://www.endslaverynow.org/freedom-house

*Canadian resources:*

Comprehensive list of organisations by province:

https://www2.gov.bc.ca/gov/content/justice/criminal-justice/victims-of-crime/humantrafficking/human-trafficking-training/resources/national-organizations

https://www.publicsafety.gc.ca/cnt/cntrng-crm/hmn-trffckng/index-en.aspx

https://www.canadiancentretoendhumantrafficking.
ca/nationalhotline/
Phone number: 1-833-900-1010

https://www.hoperestoredcanada.org/resources

https://owjn.org/human-trafficking-and-the-law/
resources/

*UK resources:*

https://www.humantraffickingfoundation.org/
support-services
Phone number: 020 3773 2040

https://www.modernslaveryhelpline.org/

https://www.stopthetraffik.org/help-and-support/

https://www.unseenuk.org/working-with-survivors/

https://harbourchurchuk.org/vista/
Vista is an outreach and support service in
Portsmouth, Gosport and the Isle of Wight, for
women involved in the sex industry past or present.
The team offers one-to-one meet ups for: a chance
to talk; help with safety planning and next steps;
advocacy and referrals to other specialist support.
Vista runs weekly wellbeing groups for women who
have experienced violence and abuse.

*Global initiatives:*

https://www.a21.org/

https://www.stopthetraffik.org/

https://gaatw.org/

https://love146.org/mission-vision/

https://healtrafficking.org/resources/end-child-prostitution-and-trafficking-ecpat/

https://ecpat.org/

https://sharedhope.org/

*Documentaries:*

*Nefarious* by Exodus Cry (available on YouTube) https://www.youtube.com/watch?v=MFaDHgXPbUg&ab_channel=ExodusCry

*I am Jane Doe* (available on Netflix)

*Brides and Brothels: The Rohingya Trade* (2018) (available on YouTube) https://www.youtube.com/watch?v=rP3zc6bEQsg&ab_channel=AlJazeeraEnglish

*Sex Trafficking in America* (available on PBS) https://www.pbs.org/wgbh/frontline/film/sex-trafficking-in-america/

———————— ✦ ————————

Beyond Support is a remote telephone support service, offering free, confidential emotional and practical support to women currently or previously involved in selling sex. They offer a women-centred, trauma-informed service for up to eighteen months, as well as up to twenty free counselling sessions for women they support.

www.beyondthestreets.org.uk

———————— ✦ ————————

## Additional Support:

*Unseen UK*
Bristol (National Reach)

Website: www.unseenuk.org

Support Provided:
- Safehouses for women survivors of trafficking
- 24/7 Modern Slavery & Exploitation Helpline (08000 121 700)
- Advocacy, casework and rehabilitation support

*Medaille Trust*
National (Headquartered in London & Manchester)

Website: www.medaille-trust.org.uk

Support Provided:
- Safe accommodation
- Trauma-informed recovery services
- Outreach and support for victims of modern slavery and sexual exploitation

## *The Sophie Hayes Foundation*

London (National Programs)

Website: www.sophiehayesfoundation.org

Support Provided:

- Employability workshops for survivors
- Confidence-building and life-skills development
- Long-term support to reduce re-trafficking risk

## *Women@theWell*

London

Website: www.watw.org.uk

Support Provided:

- Specialised services for women in prostitution and those affected by trafficking
- Drop-in centre, mental health support, and harm reduction
- Immigration and criminal justice advocacy